I0145332

15 days
of prayer with

SAINT
PIER GIORGIO FRASSATI

15 days
of prayer / series

On a journey, it's good to have a guide. Even great saints took spiritual directors or confessors with them on their itineraries toward sanctity. Now you can be guided by the most influential spiritual figures of all time. The 15 Days of Prayer series introduces their deepest and most personal thoughts.

This popular series is perfect if you are looking for a gift, or if you want to be introduced to a particular guide and his or her spirituality. Each volume contains:

- ଔ A brief biography of the saint or spiritual leader
- ଔ A guide to creating a format for prayer or retreat
- ଔ Fifteen meditation sessions with reflection guides

15 days
of prayer with

Saint
Pier Giorgio Frassati

Fr. Charles Desjobert, OP

NCP
NEW CITY PRESS

Published in the United States by New City Press
136 Madison Avenue, Floors 5 & 6,
PMB #4290 New York, NY 10016
www.newcitypress.com

© 2025 New City Press (English translation)

Translated from the original French edition
Prier 15 jours avec Pier Giorgio Frassati
© 2024 Groupe Elidia
Editions Nouvelle Cité
10 rue Mercœur, 75011 Paris
www.nouvellecite.fr

15 days of prayer with Saint Pier Giorgio Frassati
Fr. Charles Desjobert, OP

Library of Congress Control Number: 2025935470

ISBN: 978-1-56548-718-5 paperback
ISBN: 978-1-56548-719-2 e-book

Printed in the United States of America

Contents

Introduction

Who Is Pier Giorgio?

*P*ier Giorgio was born on April 6, 1901, into a well-to-do family in Turin. His father, Alfredo Frassati, was the founder and owner of *La Stampa*, one of Italy's leading daily newspapers. Adelaide, his mother, was a painter. His only sister, Luciana, was born a year after him. Family life was not straightforward: His authoritarian and strict parents showed little love. As a child, Pier Giorgio was joyful, if also stubborn, sometimes shutting himself off in total silence. He was impetuous—you could say, incorrigible—and fights with his sister were not uncommon.

Pier Giorgio's time was divided between Turin and the family villa at Pollone, about 40 miles to the north, nestled under the Alps and close to the Marian shrine of Oropa. He was very young when he first discovered the mountains. His love for the snowy heights would never stop growing. Walking and climbing, treading new paths along rock faces still out of his reach—all this was the stuff of his dreams. There, way up high, he would sing his heart out, always a little out of tune, but who cares!

The Turin that Pier Giorgio knew was growing rapidly—a rich industrial city, but with squalid slums as far as the eye could see. Turin could dazzle the world as it welcomed the Universal Exhibition, in 1911. It was, however, the poverty of the workers that struck Pier Giorgio. One morning, opening the door to a child who was barefoot and begging, he immediately untied his shoes and handed them over. Such caring deeds toward those who suffered would become ever more frequent in his teenage years.

Giorgio—as Pier Giorgio was also called (but never just "Pier")—was homeschooled in his early years, taking his exams with the Salesians. He then continued his education in a state school, along with his sister. It did not work out well: He misbehaved and got expelled twice. So his parents moved him to the Jesuit *Istituto Sociale*, in the autumn of 1913, to avoid his having to repeat a school year. Alfredo was disappointed in his son, whom he thought of as worse than useless.

When the war broke out in 1914, Pier Giorgio, the son of a senator, found himself caught up in the arguments between supporters and opponents of Italy's neutrality—to the point of being excluded from some lecture courses because of his father's views. He was horrified by the total devastation of war. So there grew in him a great desire for peace, a peace built upon more than merely human justice. True peace would require something more from us, something even more beautiful: to answer evil with good. When his bicycle got stolen, he simply reacted: *"Perhaps it was someone who needed it more than me!"* In 1923, he was appalled by the French occupation of the Ruhr and the exorbitant reparations taking their toll on Germany. Such injustice could only lead to further war.

At home, he found little support for his faith: Though his grandmother was very devout, his father was agnostic, and his mother practiced mostly out of social habit. And yet, Pier Giorgio deepened his personal prayer life, especially through the Rosary. He received Holy Communion daily, despite his parents' worrying that he might become a *bigotto*, "holier-than-thou." Pier Giorgio asked himself whether he might be called to the priesthood—maybe as a missionary? —but he felt that becoming a priest in Italy at that time risked cutting himself off from the poorest and from wider society. He was to find another way to give his life.

Early in 1921, his father was sent as ambassador to Berlin and settled there with his wife and Luciana. Remaining alone in Turin, Pier Giorgio made several trips to Germany, a place he loved very much. But high society life held no appeal for him. While his sister enjoyed the receptions at the embassy, he would make himself scarce, spending his time with the less fortunate. This pained his father, who had hoped that Pier Giorgio would take up the family newspaper and assume his place among the great and the good of postwar Italy. The ambassador observed with bitterness that his son was following another path. But which? He had no idea.

Pier Giorgio then made the acquaintance of Fr. Carl Sonnenschein (1876–1929), nicknamed the "St. Francis of Berlin." This maverick priest and founder of a Catholic student movement lived the Gospel values with remarkable integrity, including a keen social commitment. Long hours visiting the poor with Fr. Sonnenschein left a lasting mark on the young man.

His stays in Germany increased his desire to become a mining engineer. Having attended some classes at the Polytechnic University of Turin from 1918 onward, in the early 1920s, Pier Giorgio enrolled in a civil engineering degree course. But the studies were a real chore; it took him enormous willpower just to stay at his desk. This was hardly surprising since Pier Giorgio was otherwise doing a bit too much. He had joined all sorts of societies: He was a member of The Italian Federation of Catholic Universities [*Federazione Universitaria Cattolica Italiana*, or FUCI], in the *Cesare Balbo* circle; he took part in the Italian Alpine Club [CAI] and joined many young adults' groups, Eucharistic congresses, prayer vigils, and so on.

His student life could have been anyone else's. Unremarkable, then? And yet . . . from the age of seventeen, he had been a member of the Society of St. Vincent de Paul and regularly visited the marginalized. The rendezvous was at 6 p.m. at the foot of the bell tower of the Church of Our Lady of Consolation (*la Consolata*). From there, he would walk down Via Santa Chiara, attend to the sick at the Cottolengo Hospital, and care for the elderly in the neighboring hospices.

So, from that time onward, he impressed people with his joyfulness, his purity, his humility, his simplicity, and his faith. Many spoke of his good example and regarded him with astonishment and admiration. They were struck by his attitude: determined and courageous, authentic and generous. And yet, Pier Giorgio kept quiet about all he did. Humbly he served, at ease with everyone, no matter their condition. And his humility did not cramp his style: It made his way of life more contagious.

His desire to follow Christ blossomed into a fuller commitment. On May 28, 1922, aged twenty-one, Pier Giorgio became a Lay Dominican in the Church of St. Dominic, in Turin. He took the name Brother Girolamo (Jerome) in honor of the Dominican friar, Girolamo Savonarola, whose ardor and determination appealed to him. He also deepened his faith through reading his favorite authors: St. Paul, St. Augustine, St. Thomas Aquinas, and of course, Dante, of whom he could quote entire stanzas. From then on, his letters began to teem with references to these writers. *The Dialogue* of St. Catherine of Siena, which he particularly loved, would inspire him in his adult years.

His activities were not limited to good deeds but also included political activism. Pier Giorgio took part in meetings of the Catholic trade unions, meeting the workers, and it was not uncommon to see him at the factory gates during strikes, defending the employees against pressure from Communist leagues. He signed up with the Italian People's Party despite his father's disapproval. When the Fascists took power in October 1922, Pier Giorgio persevered in his Catholic political activism. Although his participation in religious processions earned him a great deal of ridicule, he did not hesitate to join them. It even cost him some hours in police custody. He understood the dangers of Fascism and, when the politicians of the People's Party joined Mussolini's government, he was profoundly disappointed. His opposition came to a head when the Frassati family home was attacked by Fascists in June 1924. It was a rare moment of appreciation from his family: Pier Giorgio's bravery was praised by all, even as far as a mention in *The Times* of London.

In his spiritual life, Pier Giorgio relied on invaluable friendships. With his best friend, Marco Beltramo, and six other young men and women, he founded the Society of Shady Characters (*Tipi Loschi*), on the occasion of a memorable mountain climb, May 18, 1924. A mixed group of men and women was unusual for that period, but they met around common interests in sports, prayer, and simple fun. They did not take themselves very seriously. Pier Giorgio gained the nickname Robespierre, for a laugh, and the letters they exchanged were enlivened with "cannon shots" expressing their sheer joy.

Among the members of the Society of Shady Characters, there was one Pier Giorgio fell in love with—Laura Hidalgo. He tried to introduce this young woman, an orphan from humbler origins, to his family. But he realized, sorrowfully, that he would not be able to marry her: His parents would never give their consent. Thus began a very dark period for him, as witnessed in his letters: How could he live through this renunciation?

The year 1925 began with the opening of the Jubilee doors by Pope Pius XI in Rome. This Holy Year, Pier Giorgio's last on earth, would be decisive. His sister's marriage to a Polish diplomat on January 24, which took her away from the family, was a real wrench for both siblings. Pier Giorgio remained alone in a family that was falling apart: His parents' recurring

arguments had little by little transformed into
silent warfare. They were on the brink of separation. Along with all this came the end of his
studies and difficult life choices ahead. It's at
this time that he wrote his most beautiful letters,
those in which joy resurfaces after the storm.
Despite the rough going, he had an interior
certainty: He wanted to serve God through his
brothers and sisters. It was full of this confidence
that Pier Giorgio died suddenly, on Saturday,
July 4, 1925, aged twenty-four, carried off by
a violent bout of polio. No one had suspected
anything . . . just a bit of fever, that's all. His
grandmother was dying at that time, and all eyes
were on her. As in life, so in death, Pier Giorgio
went unknown by his own kin. And yet his
charity was alive right to his last moments. At
his burial, hundreds of people turned out from
all sections of society, especially the poorest.
And so the truth came out about the immense
love of Pier Giorgio, a model of how to live the
Gospel for all.

Preface to the English Edition

*P*ier Giorgio is one of those fiery, passionate souls who keeps his eyes on the prize. Convinced that he cannot merely get along but that he must live to the full, he set out on the demanding way of the Gospel. His life was lived beautifully, in service of the weakest and in humility. This simple and true gift of self, inhabited by a deep joy, was something he achieved in barely twenty-four years.

Pier Giorgio did not keep a spiritual diary. Most of his writing consists of letters to his friends or his sister. In reading them through and letting them recount to us the beauty of his love for all, we discover who this young adult from Turin was. In addition to his writings, we have hundreds of little anecdotes, like the *fioretti* of St. Francis, which bear witness to Giorgio's charity in action. To discover the faith that inspires Pier Giorgio, we will also walk with the saints he was particularly fond of—St. Paul and St. Augustine, St. Thomas Aquinas and St. Catherine of Siena—but also Dante and his *Divine Comedy.* Extracts from the Psalms, which we sing morning, noon, and night in the Divine Office, will be like little prayers to uplift our meditation throughout the book.

I must admit that writing this book on (and with!) Pier Giorgio was no easy task. Firstly, because I'm not a writer, and maybe also because Pier Giorgio wasn't either! No long treatise on theology, no splendid spiritual ideas: He did not preach by writing, but it is rather through his whole life that he evangelizes us.

His deeply interior life was constantly challenged by the needs of others. As a Dominican friar, I have been particularly touched by this young lad who goes out to meet everyone and who sees in everyone, whatever kind of poverty they suffer, a child loved by God. Pier Giorgio always acts with great humility, and I hope I have been able to convey in these pages his simplicity, his enthusiasm, and his warmth, too. His life is a reminder that one is not born a saint but one becomes a saint by grace and by perseverance: "Not that I have already obtained this or am already perfect; but I press on to make it my own, because Christ Jesus has made me his own. Brethren, I do not consider that I have made it on my own; but one thing I do, forgetting what lies behind and straining forward to what lies ahead, I press on toward the goal for the prize of the upward call of God in Christ Jesus" (Phil 3:12-14).

There are many people, "shady characters" or not, who pray to Pier Giorgio and have taken him as a companion for the journey in the footsteps of Christ. Among the many benefits attributed to his intercession, two healings have been recognized as miracles, confirming the shining sanctity of his life. In 1933, Domenico Sellan was completely and definitively restored to health after having had a terminal diagnosis of bone tuberculosis. In 2011, the young Kevin Becker, who had suffered an extremely serious head injury, was healed without any aftereffects at all. The canonization of Pier Giorgio in 2025, exactly a century after his death, is the ultimate recognition that his Christian witness is ever relevant to everyone, everywhere.

I would like to thank Wanda Gawronska, Pier Giorgio's niece, for her numerous clarifications and her easygoing hospitality in Pollone. Thank you to my brethren in the English Dominican Province, especially to Fr. Matthew Jarvis and Fr. Joseph Bailham, remembering fondly our days walking in the footsteps of Pier Giorgio in Turin and Oropa. Thank you, Matthew, for your translation—a marathon effort to convert my poor French into such elegant English!

Finally, thank you, Pier Giorgio, you who are drawing us to the heights when we seem to get stuck in the mud. I entrust you with the call

to holiness of Clément, the youngest of my four
nieces and nephews, of my godchildren Louise,
Athénaïs, and Antonin, and of each one of us.

Abbreviations

*A*ll passages in italics are the spoken words or writings of Pier Giorgio. In the case of extracts from letters, the date indicated is the date of writing. For the other quotations and episodes of Pier Giorgio's life, an acronym or surname followed by a page number refers to the works below.

SIC: Christina Siccardi, *Pier Giorgio Frassati: A Hero for our Times*. Translated by Michael J. Miller. Ignatius Press, 2016.

LFC: Luciana Frassati, *La charité de Pier Giorgio, mon frère*. Conquistador, 1953.

LFJ: Luciana Frassati, *Pier Giorgio Frassati: Les jours de sa vie*. Le Sarment-Fayard, 1990.

COD: Marino Codi, *Pier Giorgio Frassati, una valanga di vita*. Portalupi, 2001.

The passages from the Bible or other classic books loved by Pier Giorgio are indicated using standard references after the following abbreviations.

Confessions: St. Augustine, *Confessions.* Translated by R. S. Pine-Coffin. Penguin, 1961.

Dialogue: St. Catherine of Siena, *The Dialogue.* The Classics of Western Spirituality. Translated by Suzanne Noffke, OP. SPCK Publishing, 1980.

Paradiso: Dante, *The Divine Comedy, 3: Paradiso.* Translated by John D. Sinclair. Oxford University Press, 1939.

Summa: St. Thomas Aquinas, *Summa Theologiæ.* Translated by Fathers of the English Dominican Province. Second and revised edition. Burns Oates and Washbourne, 1920–1922.

Translator's Note

*T*his translation follows the French text, except when citing from English editions of works noted above. Biblical citations have been taken from the Revised Standard Version: Catholic Edition, with the Psalms from the Grail Psalter (using the Greek/Latin numbering). Citations from Pier Giorgio's letters have been freshly translated from the original Italian. For further reading, consult the English edition of *Pier Giorgio Frassati: Letters to His Friends and Family*, translated by Fr. Timothy E. Deeter, and edited by Fr. Timothy E. Deeter and Christine M. Wohar, St. Pauls, 2009.

I would like to extend my own thanks to Frère Charles for having written this marvelous little book and for his friendship since our early years in the Dominican Order. Fr. Joseph Bailham, OP, was the first to introduce me to Pier Giorgio as a real friend, for which I will always be deeply grateful. My heartfelt thanks also go to Br. Vincent Löning, OP, who worked with me on the earliest drafts, and to Dr. Paige dePolo, who very kindly read the whole script and helped me refine it on many points.

1

To the Heights

I left my heart on those mountains with the hope of finding it again this summer when making the ascent of Mont Blanc. (March 4, 1923)

Sunday was one of those magnificent days and, from the top of the glacier, my thoughts ran to faraway friends; I would have wanted them all here to enjoy together with me that marvelous spectacle. The last stretch was the most entertaining because we made the ascent to the peak from the side where the rocks were steeper, but at the same time more solid. And now I must not think any longer of these beautiful things and regrettably apply myself again to thermal engineering. . . . Again, a thousand thanks for your pickaxe which has served me very well. (July 9, 1923)

*P*ier Giorgio was athletic. He enjoyed horse riding and sea excursions. He practiced a bit of fencing, cycling, and especially skiing. But, far and away, he preferred climbing mountains. Approaching the snow-capped peaks, he ascended toward higher and purer places with breathtaking scenery, where he could contemplate the Creator.

Nailed here and there on the back of his bedroom door, poems evoked his love of mountains. From his window, he could see them stretching away into the distance. *"With every passing day, I am falling madly in love with the mountains; their fascination attracts me"* (SIC 258). The mountains echoed back the declaration of his love for God: *"Mountains, mountains, mountains, I love you!"* (SIC 260): love of the infinite, of the purity and simplicity of these great open horizons; love of freedom to be won and of the new challenges that spring up at every point; love, too, of the men and women on whom one relies to reach the goal. Climbing steep mountains is never a solitary task: There is no hike without a team and a rope that holds, supports, and protects you. He knew that, in the mountains, one has to be able to rely on others, and that is also how he found happiness.

Conscious of what a blessing it was to have such a strong physical constitution, Pier Giorgio lived his passion to the full: *"See how important good health can be! . . . Our good health must be put at*

the service of those who lack it, as otherwise we would
be betraying the very gift of God and his Providence"
(LFC 214). So many people suffer in their bodies,
so Pier Giorgio, in the full flush of health, did not
wish to waste his good fortune. His body was a
means to give thanks to the Creator. When soul
and body work together, the person becomes
great, upright, and closer to God. That is why
Pier Giorgio loved sports, especially the kind
that pushes us upward, whether in the heat of
the day or the fresh air of the great starry night.

How did he discover this so early on in life?
Our flesh so often feels heavy and burdensome,
but he understood that the love of God can
spread into our body. The athletic Pier Giorgio
was well ahead of his time and a breath of fresh
air in that still quite puritan period of the early
twentieth century. He reminds us of the newness
of the Christian message, which affirms that the
body and the soul go together. If God became
incarnate in Jesus Christ, if we believe in the
resurrection of the body, it is because the body
is precious and good. Mountaineering taught
Pier Giorgio that the soul sustains the suffering
body during those steep hikes. And that body,
which expressed itself freely in sports, gave his
sometimes-melancholic soul a real taste for this
space and time in which God has planted us.

Pier Giorgio did not use his physical capaci-
ties only for himself. Despite enjoying a challenge, he did not take part in the race undertaken

—not without fatalities—by European nations in the interwar period to conquer the highest Alpine peaks. Although he could boast of his exploits, he preferred to organize expeditions with less able friends. In first position on the rope, he was also the first to stop when one of his friends ran out of breath. Instantly, without being asked, he would cheer his friend up and add their baggage to his own. He might even hand over his own coat, as his friend Riccardo Bordi recalled: "I put on the cape that he had immediately lent to me when he learned that I lacked one and would not have been able to participate in the excursion. I had accepted, thinking he had another, but then he was left without one. *'As you see,'* he told me, *'I am not cold!'*" (SIC 265).

Reaching the summit, he would pray the *De profundis* (Psalm 129) for anyone who had died in the mountains. He would then give thanks openly to God, in a moment of recollection and joy in the gentle breeze: *"When you go into the mountains the first task is to set your own conscience straight, because you don't know if you will ever come back. Yet despite all this, I am not afraid, but desire more than ever to climb mountains, to conquer the most daring peaks, to experience that pure joy which is only to be found in the mountains"* (August 13, 1923). When he went climbing and braved such adventures, it was not to look down on others nor to stand out from the crowd. Up there, he could present himself just as he was before the Lord. Short of breath in the difficult terrain, his hands sweaty, but always with the smile of one who loves and knows he is loved, high up there before a wide vista, he would stand in awe of the goodness of the Creator.

The mountains are not a place of merely human achievement. They are also the place of God's activity. He reveals himself there, as he has done throughout Biblical history: in the thunder or the gentle breeze, from Mount Sinai all the way to Golgotha. Pier Giorgio was nourished by this since, for him, a mountain was the place where self-knowledge was gained, friendship was founded, and faith established itself on the rock—finding oneself, meeting a friend, and discovering God—a place where one lives only to love, and where only the passion for the good remains. "How beautiful upon the mountains are the feet of him who brings good tidings, who publishes peace, who brings good tidings of good, who publishes salvation, who says to Sion, 'Your God reigns' " (Is 52:7).

Pier Giorgio always opened a way forward. When faced with a wall, when the rock face made the ascent impossible, when blocks obstructed the path, he would attempt a breakthrough. Where we would see an insurmountable barrier, he looked for the breach, the way upward. When the cliff crumbled, his hand found another grip among the frozen stones.

To go forward, testing the best holds and finding new ones when they fail, as we are asked to do by the prophet Jeremiah: "Stand by the roads, and look, and ask for the ancient paths, where the good way is; and walk in it, and find rest for your souls" (Jer 6:16). It is in this ascent that he leads us: Let us seek with him the handhold or grip that will enable us to pull ourselves up when all seems lost. And when we start to slip, we are reassured by a solid rope linking us to a friend above, ready to rescue us.

A few days before he died, on the back of the last photo we have of him, Pier Giorgio wrote: *"Verso l'alto"* (To the heights). This photo shows him climbing a mountain—his last ascent, his last words—a motto for life!

Discussion Questions

Do I get outside much and am I grateful for contact with the natural world?

Where in nature do I feel most at peace? Why?

Spend some time reading and meditating on Psalm 103 ("Bless the Lord, my soul"). When have I been most awed by the beauty of nature? What is there in nature that makes me realize God is Creator?

What place does my body have in my spiritual awareness?

2

Ready to Serve

The apostolate of charity means going among those who suffer and comforting them . . . for the Catholic religion is based on charity, which is none other than the most perfect Love. St. Paul the Apostle says, "The charity of Christ urges us on" [2 Cor 5:14], and without this fire—which, little by little, must destroy our personality [our selfishness] *in order to make our hearts beat only for the sufferings of others—we would not be Christians, and Catholics even less.* (July 29, 1923)

As Catholics, we have a Love which surpasses all others and, after that which is owed to God, is immensely beautiful, as beautiful as our religion. A Love which had as an advocate the Apostle [Paul], *who preached it every day in all his letters to the various Faithful. That Charity without which, as St. Paul says, every other virtue is useless. That alone can be a guide and direction for a whole life, for a whole program.* (March 6, 1925)

No half-measures with Pier Giorgio! See this young man, full of brilliant future promise and all the potential to be a successful social climber, crossing the wretched neighborhoods of Turin in shirtsleeves. There's work to be done. A stone's throw away from the rich neighborhoods, there's sprawling poverty and suffering. That much hasn't changed! "The poor you always have with you . . . " (Jn 12:8). And it's very much among them that Christ is present, until the end of time.

Following the principles of respectable Italian society, the young Giorgio learned to "do charity"—a performative generosity, where the benefactor always tends to put themselves on show. But the charity of Pier Giorgio went far beyond that. As a loving act, under the sign of Christ, it discovered in the weakest person a brother or sister. It didn't worry about knowing whether it was mistaken or not. It was a gift, without strings attached. The street kid that I pass in the subway station, the smelly old man dozing off on a street corner, the young lady stretching out a cupped hand at the church doors, are these not our brothers, our sisters? "As you did it to one of the least of these my brethren, you did it to me" (Mt 25:40). Pier Giorgio saw in everyone a person to be loved. And he didn't hesitate. That's what was so disarming about him: Without mixed motives, he didn't run off a list of the many reasons that might justify doing nothing. *Caritas Christi urget nos*—"The love of Christ urges us on" (2 Cor 5:14)—is still inscribed above the entrance to the Cottolengo Hospital where Pier Giorgio found his brothers and sisters. He ran because love had gripped him. And that is how the Kingdom of God comes among us.

In sportswear befitting an explorer or factory worker more than an aristocrat, Pier Giorgio frequented the most notorious locations. The Cottolengo Hospital was a truly repellent place, where all kinds of poverty were compounded, from physical decrepitude to mental health problems. Yet, he was not repelled. When a friend asked him how he overcame his disgust among such filthy houses that greeted him with foul odors, he responded, *"We should never forget that, although the house is dirty, it is toward Christ that we go. . . . Around sick people, around the needy, I see a particular light, a light which we ourselves lack"* (LFC 41). Pier Giorgio did not seek out the fortunate ones but turned toward those who needed him. It didn't matter whether they were respectable or not; here was a truly universal brotherliness. And this love was not disembodied: Pier Giorgio went so far as to give the injections himself, in the suffering flesh of those he met in the hospice. He would go there at a brisk pace, slipping hastily inside to meet God in the poor, just as he met the poor in God. For Frassati, love of God and love of neighbor formed a single flame, which could not be distinguished. This fire, received in prayer, enabled him to become a light to his brothers and sisters.

"What have you that you did not receive?" St. Paul asked (1 Cor 4:7). With him, Pier Giorgio knew that he had received everything gratuitously. This made him free and enabled him to give in turn. Nothing was to be hoarded jealously. If everything is a gift to us, everything is ours to be given to another. And who is this other? "Who is my neighbor?" (Lk 10:29). *"Jesus comes to visit me every day in Communion, and for me to visit the poor who belong to him is the very least I can do in return"* (LFC 21). There's my neighbor! The one whom I approach in the communion of goods, both material and spiritual. Otherwise, the one who knocks at the door would always remain a stranger. To give of ourselves, to find that we are the ones who received all: what freedom! Yet this did not prevent Pier Giorgio from painfully realizing, *"I who have received so many things from God, have remained always so negligent, so bad, while those who have not been privileged like me are so infinitely better than me"* (February 1922). Was this despondency? No, it was simple humility, the sort which can keep putting us back on track.

Born into a rich family, he made himself poor. He would dig so deep into his own funds that he deprived himself in order to help those in need. To a friend who suggested having a drink, he replied: *"Let's give to a poor person what we would spend on drink, and our thirst will pass"* (LFC 31). He would save up, without hesitating to become a beggar. On occasion, having greased the boots of the whole company before an Alpine climb, Pier Giorgio would simply extend his hand with the plea: *"And what will you give me for this?"* (LFC 55). Giving, for him, was as simple as breathing. As he breathed his last, it was again fraternal love for others that moved him. It was a Friday, the usual day for visiting the poor with the St. Vincent de Paul Society. He handed his sister a little scrap of paper, in handwriting rendered practically illegible by his paralysis. She deciphered there his final act of charity: instructions to buy medicines for a sick man—a last act of concern for those he loved so much. Never a stranger to the families he aided, he was received by them as a brother or a father. And, right to the end, he remained a brother to those in need.

Pier Giorgio made it his rule to remain anonymous, as much as possible. He considered it essential not to embarrass others by making a show of his own good works. Such acts were but a human duty. That was why, one day, he criticized a friend who thought he was helping by revealing Giorgio's good deed: *"That evening, you broke your promise not to reveal the one who had done this very small act of charity"* (LFC 29). On a visit to a poor family, Pier Giorgio asked almost trivially, *"This child, how much milk does he take*

each day? . . . Half a liter? Ah! Okay" (LFC 70).
That seemed to be the end of the matter, and he
didn't announce, as other people would, "We
will bring you the milk!" But he would bring it
as soon as possible. And when he mentioned his
poor brothers and sisters to his friends, it was to
get their advice, not to show off. "Love is patient
and kind; love is not jealous or boastful; it is not
arrogant or rude . . . but rejoices in the right.
Love bears all things, believes all things, hopes
all things, endures all things. Love never ends"
(1 Cor 13:4-8).

Discussion Questions

Do I worry about money a lot?

Do I have more possessions than I need?

How do I respond when faced with people in
dire poverty?

What gifts do I possess that I could share more
willingly with others?

Who are the needy in my neighborhood, and
what can I do for them?

3

Always Joyful

You ask me if I'm joyful, and how could I not be? As long as the Faith will give me strength: always joyful! No Catholic can be anything but joyful; sadness must be banished from Catholic souls. Pain is not the same as sadness, which is a sickness worse than any other. This sickness is nearly always produced by atheism. But the goal for which we have been created shows us the path, no matter how strewn with many thorns—but not a sad path. It is joyful, even through the pains of life. (February 14, 1925)

Joy is not a matter of fine words. *"Most esteemed Madam President. Pray, do not expect from me an epistle in the style of the fourteenth century. We miserable mortals, plunged as we are in arid and abstruse mathematical problems, cannot (alas!) slake our thirst at the pure fountains of the beautiful Italian style, but you, whom I know to be so indulgent, will have compassion"* (July 20, 1924). The stage is set! Pier Giorgio did not write great treatises about joy. Rather he dared to live it daily, through his humor, his simplicity, and his freedom.

As a boy, Pier Giorgio appeared joyful in a nevertheless somber life. His cheerfulness might have seemed superficial had it not been born from the struggles of his adolescent and adult life. Some people were fooled. Wasn't his joy simply the fruit of his perfect health and privileged social standing? In reality, his joy emanated primarily from his uprightness, interior faithfulness, and immense trust in God. It grew progressively, in the midst of suffering and adversity. It burst forth like rare roses among thorns—and what roses!

In a bourgeois society, where cheerfulness is not the number one value, Pier Giorgio let the words of the Apostle Paul ring out in his life: "Rejoice in the Lord always; again I will say, Rejoice!" (Phil 4:4). This kind of joy is life-giving and, when it is missing, the whole person is disfigured. Pier Giorgio noticed that in the slums of Turin, among the poorest of the poor. He noticed it even more among the well-off families of Turin's high society, in his own house no less. His sister depicted the family atmosphere in this way: "The terrace without flowers that joined it to the dining room and the fireplace without a fire seemed to be the symbol of our family" (SIC 29). Pier Giorgio's parents were on the brink of separation, his sister didn't understand him, his studies were tedious, and he realized bitterly that, in the Church no less, joy was neglected. This did not crush him. In this world invaded by sadness, he offered his cheerfulness as the best remedy: *"And your life, how's it going? Mine, as you can tell from the beginning of this letter, is going through possibly the most acute phase of a serious crisis and it's just at this time that my sister is going far away. So it's up to me to remain cheerful at home and to dissipate the gloomy atmosphere produced by all these problems piling up on me"* (January 15, 1925).

The source of Christian joy is twofold. It is born from the assurance that God loves us and comes to save us, and it grows in the amazing trust that God shows toward humanity: "I have helped you; I have kept you and given you as a covenant to the people, to establish the land, to apportion the desolate heritages; saying to the prisoners, 'Come forth,' to those who are in darkness, 'Appear!' " (Is 49:8-9). The Lord comes to lead his people into light, and Christ trusts us to be the transmitters of his inexhaustible love. He is not afraid to entrust us with this huge task, and his joy overflows in the Gospel: "Rejoice, be joyful!" Pier Giorgio, despite his imperfections, humbly accepted what the Lord was calling him to: being happy to live. Does he desire anything different for us? Are we not freed? Why do we just stand there, as if we were still afraid? Joy bursts forth in the Psalms, which speak of this liberation: "When the Lord delivered Sion from bondage, it seemed like a dream. Then was our mouth filled with laughter, on our lips there were songs. The heathens themselves said: 'What marvels the Lord worked for them!' What marvels the Lord worked for us! Indeed, we were glad!'" (Ps 125:1-3). If Pier Giorgio could bear witness to his joy with such power, it was because he had discovered the true face of God, who did not come to condemn the world, but that the world might be saved through him (cf. Jn 3:16).

" 'What can bring us happiness?' many say. Lift up the light of your face on us, O Lord. You have put into my heart a greater joy than they have from abundance of corn and new wine" (Ps 4:7-8). Pier Giorgio realized that joy could not come from the abundance of material possessions. For him, joy comes through contemplating creation, the snowy peaks, the flowering fields in the Alps, and the dark greens of the forests of Piedmont: *"Every day, I'm falling more and more in love with the mountains and, if only my studies allowed, I would spend whole days on the mountains to contemplate, in that pure air, the Greatness of the Creator"* (August 6, 1923). Nature continuously revealed to him the loving face of God.

Joy is thus a gift that one cannot keep for oneself, yet our world is greedy to do so. To be honest, I've often got the impression that we are wary of joy. Isn't joy a cover-up for something else? Isn't it a facile cure? Pier Giorgio believed that joy was the best means to proclaim that Christ was alive: "Light shines forth for the just, and joy for the upright of heart" (Ps 96:11).

Hence, his cheerfulness can be seen in his letters, which are full of fresh air. He also loved to bring a festive atmosphere to the gatherings of students, not hesitating to make his powerful voice ring out or to frankly burst out laughing. So, for many of his friends, his simple cheerfulness offered a space to recharge themselves. Tinged with the experience of his toughest interior struggles, his cheerfulness could be adapted to each person: "Rejoice with those who rejoice, weep with those who weep" (Rom 12:15).

If *"God has divided our life in a very good way, making joy alternate with serious moments"* (7 March 1923), God also knows how to speak to us with humor. The limpid humor of Pier Giorgio had something to do with true joy because it aimed at the good. It was with this joyful air that he recounted a memorable evening with the Shady Characters:

> *The lunch (without wishing to boast) went extremely well and was consumed in perfect joy. To tell the truth, the guests were poorly welcomed by the chef* [Pier Giorgio] *because they arrived punctually a half hour late, which meant that I was not accountable for the dryness of the pasta. When lunch was over, we sang our beautiful songs of the mountains, among others, then the Terror* [again Pier Giorgio!] *went out to get a breath of fresh air.* (August 6, 1924)

Discussion Questions

Who are the people, and what are the activities, that bring me most joy? Why is that?

How do I understand St. Paul's instruction to be "always joyful"?

In the dull and uninspiring parts of my life, how can I become more cheerful?

Do I rejoice in doing the right thing, even when it brings me no material advantage?

4

The Shady Characters

Dearest Friend,

*It's now two days since I left Villa Santa Croce,
where I thought a lot about you. Your spirit
was present between those walls where we had
spent such beautiful days together. . . . In this
earthly life, after affection for parents and sisters, one of the most beautiful affections is that
of friendship; and I ought to thank God every
day for having given me such good friends, men
and women, who constitute a precious guide
for me throughout my whole life. . . . I'm send-
ing you my best wishes, or even just one. But I
believe it's the only one that a true friend can
offer to a dear friend, and it is this: May the
peace of the Lord be with you always, for if you
possess that peace every day, you will be truly
rich. Heartfelt salutations in Jesus Christ.*
(April 10, 1925)

*T*his letter to Marco Beltramo undoubtedly provides us with one of the most characteristic traits of Pier Giorgio's sanctity. This friendship grabbed me as soon as I encountered it—a generous friendship that knows no bounds. Pier Giorgio makes us discover the power and the joy of the deep friendships he built around him.

He first experienced this friendship with the young people of his age in the university circle *Cesare Balbo*, in the St. Vincent de Paul group, and in the Alpine club. The atmosphere there was fraternal, joyful, and full of humor. And it was in this spirit that he created the Society of Shady Characters, a group of about a dozen friends who organized mountaineering trips and sent one another letters that were deliberately pompous and would end with astonishing greetings: *"Citizen Robespierre sends you terrorist cannon shots, boom!"* (June 13, 1924).

Friends? Or rather a band of wannabe-revolutionary shady characters . . . One evening, attending a theater production, with the French Revolution as backdrop, Pier Giorgio thought he could see a resemblance between one of the characters in the play, Perrault, and his friend Marco. So, the moment he met up with him the next day, he cried out, *"Perrault, you're his spitting image!"* To which Marco replied, "And you, you must be Robespierre!" (LFJ 139). The two nicknames were immediately adopted. Thus was born "the Terror," a unique and most important subsection of the Society of Shady Characters. In other words, the two of them didn't take themselves too seriously. That's the spirit! Better be *a terror* for a laugh than a fake saint.

Friendship cannot be forced but is born, a little at random, through an encounter. While purely human, friendship is wonderful because it reveals something of God. It becomes even more beautiful when it dares to anchor itself in faith: On this rock it becomes unshakable. To a friend who was about to join the army, Pier Giorgio wrote:

> *I wandered in thought to those joyous days spent together on our mountain excursions. My only consolation in the course of such joyous, yet also sad, thoughts is the certainty that a unique bond, which knows no distances, unites us and—I hope by the Grace of God—will unite us always. That is the Faith, that Common Ideal which you will be able to sustain in your career through the means given you by military life, and which I will try to defend and sustain, with God's help, in my future life as a man.*
> (November 4, 1924)

Enriched by faith and placed under the gaze of God, friendship contributes to the blossoming of our Christian vocation. It is fortified by coming into contact with the friendship that Jesus himself offers us: "No longer do I call you servants, for the servant does not know what his master is doing; but I have called you friends, for all that I have heard from my Father I have made known to you" (Jn 15:15).

Convinced of the value friendship brought to his faith, Pier Giorgio was not content to wait for it: He worked at it. He loved to build bridges with his disarming simplicity. His spontaneity touched the hearts of the people around him, even his political opponents. "He acted as he believed, spoke as he thought, and did as he said," witnessed the head of the Socialist party, Filippo Turati, bowled over by Frassati's life (SIC 329). It was with those people he felt most distant from in terms of temperament, intelligence, or social position that he spent the most time, to the astonishment of some. When a friend questioned him, "But don't you think there's a touch of fantasy in the life ideals you're lumbering yourself with?" Pier Giorgio replied with a slap on the back and an *"Of course!"* (LFC 41) —which says a lot.

But the trials of life can tarnish a friendship and disfigure it, especially if it's built on shaky foundations. How painful it is when the one we believed to be so close to us wounds us! The psalmist understands this distress: "Thus even my friend, in whom I trusted, who ate my bread, has turned against me" (Ps 40:10). Pier Giorgio discovered this requirement of friendship which, without frank honesty, will not last long.

His letters sometimes come across as sharp. In many of them, we see him reproaching a friend, readjusting a position, saying things with calmness but also firmness—without beating about the bush, a blunt stripping down! Friendship does not put up with social niceties. That's why Pier Giorgio equally dared to place his trust in his friends, to count on them, to recognize that he himself was weak and fallible. So, when he reproached a friend for having skipped an exam, he had to admit: *"Certainly, [my sermon] could come from a better pulpit, but what do you want, I'm writing to you because I'm your friend, that's all"* (August 24, 1924).

Those close to him deeply cherished his attentiveness, so full of goodness. See how one friend thanked him for a gift: "It came to me at a moment when I was about to do something stupid, and I remembered a distant friend. The thought that, despite the kilometers which separate us and our different conditions of life, the goal we aspire to is one and the same prevented me from doing the bad thing, made me happy and serene again" (LFC 164). Such friendship is *a precious guide* thanks to the power of prayer and thanks to the honesty and goodwill that unfold within it.

Also, when friends were separated by distance, he did not let the bond be weakened: *"Unfortunately, one by one, earthly friendships bring sorrows to our hearts when those we love move away, but I would like us to swear a pact that knows no earthly bounds, no limits in time: union in prayer"* (January 15, 1925).

Pier Giorgio presents himself to us as a friend and a saint. He is ready to walk with us toward the true friend—the Lord Jesus. That's what Giorgio promised us: *"Right, I will pay back my debt, that is, the one who will get to Paradise first will help the other to reach it"* (LFC 24). He is there in heaven today. Replying to a friend with whom he planned to establish a place of welcome for the elderly, Pier Giorgio exclaimed: *"You'll see, the two of us together will do great things!"* (LFC 47). He promises the same to us who take him as our traveling companion.

Discussion Questions

Who are my closest friends, and what brings us together?

How do I nurture my friendships?

What place is there for faith in my friendships with those who don't share my faith?

Have I been neglecting any friends, because of distance or some other circumstance, and what can I do today to let them know they are loved?

5

The Trials of Love

I've been in the mountains many times with Laura, many times with others. . . . Well then, my project here is to convert this special liking which I had for her, and which is not chosen, toward that end which we ought to reach, toward the light of Charity. To convert it into a respectful bond of friendship, in the Christian sense, into respect for her virtues, in imitation of her remarkable qualities, as I have for the others. You will tell me, perhaps, that it's madness to hope for this. But I believe, if you would pray a little for me, that in a short space of time I could, through prayer, achieve this state.
(March 6, 1925)

*W*hen, at age twenty-two, Pier Giorgio fell in love with Laura, he came to the painful realization that this love was fanciful. Would his mother accept that he marry this orphan from a far lower social class? Was he truly in love or

did he simply like the idea of it? It was unthink-
able that he should leave his family home while
his parents were on the brink of separation. He
talked about it with his sister. "Yesterday evening, Pier Giorgio came to my room with his
big brown eyes and told me that he was in love
with a young lady whom I know. . . . Of course,
he said nothing to Mama because that would be
the final blow. Poor boy; it was moving to hear
him speak, given his activity, which we just do
not discuss in the family. I told him to try not to
see her" (SIC 238).

Pier Giorgio knew the harshness of family
relationships. His parents did not understand
him, nor did his sister. His mother was despair-
ing of the young Pier Giorgio who could barely
string three words together: "He was scratching
himself without realizing, he couldn't write a
single line. . . . I've had enough. Sometimes I
wonder if it's a lack of intelligence and, what's
more, he's not as nice as he used to be. . . . My
God, I only wish I would die before seeing that
boy end in failure" (LFJ 27). As a young adult,
his father scolded him severely: "You must
convince yourself, dear Giorgio, that life must
be taken seriously, and the way you behave
behooves neither you nor your family, who love
you and are very disappointed by these things
which happen all too often and are repeated,
monotonous and painful. I have little hope that
you will change and yet it would be extremely

necessary to change right away. . . . Not to be living from day to day, without thinking about anything like any brainless idiot" (LFJ 92).

At home, everything turned on success and even fame. His mother thought she was flattering him when she exclaimed during a meal: "Do you know, Pier Giorgio? Don Borla told me that you've been mentioned in lectures" (LFJ 98). *"It doesn't matter at all,"* was his only reply. Such was the incomprehension that his mother concluded: "You know, talking with Pier Giorgio is a little like talking to the wind" (SIC 114).

Though we might dream of our families as being the most fertile place for love, it is not always the case. . . . Yet God has another plan. In the Bible, families are complex, patched up and undone again, more or less extended. It's not the end of the world! The Lord does not want a family to be closed in on itself, ideal, and without social failures. We have a family that we come from, just as it is. Then we have a family into which we are called. We belong indeed to a wider and more open family: the People of God. A family with many faces, and with so many sick people, poor people, and those who suffer. This is the family that Christ gathered on the roads of Galilee. When Christ's family was looking for him, he replied, "'Who is my mother, and who are my brethren?' And stretching out his hand toward his disciples, he said, 'Here are my mother and my brethren! For whoever does the will of my Father in heaven is my brother, and sister, and mother' " (Mt 12:48-50).

By recognizing God as our Father, we recognize one another as belonging to the same family: "For all who are led by the Spirit of God are sons of God. For you did not receive the spirit of slavery to fall back into fear, but you have received the spirit of sonship. When we cry, 'Abba! Father!' it is the Spirit himself bearing witness with our spirit that we are children of God" (Rom 8:14-16).

Pier Giorgio lived through an unsettled period at the end of his life as a student. Everything seemed to fall apart. And in his emotional life, he was torn between his family and his love for Laura. He found himself grappling with this delicate question: Can I exercise my freedom without destroying my family bonds? He made a choice that only he could make: He decided to stay for a while with his parents. This was a decision he placed before God with clearsightedness. But it wasn't a servile submission on his part. Pier Giorgio was not normally the sort who would let others walk over him. One day, his father was praising one of his friends: "He is such a good son that he will marry the one his father will choose" (LFJ 93). *"A true idiot then,"* Giorgio retorted without hesitation.

If Pier Giorgio resolved to reveal nothing of his love, not even to Laura, it was only after careful discernment. God never asks anything of us without having placed deep in us the desire to accomplish it. Our deepest being aspires to respond to God's will for us. And we have the wonderful assurance that the Lord wants our happiness: That is his will! This does not fall from the sky but reveals itself in the concrete situations of our lives. Listening is, therefore, of prime importance because there is no general theory in this area. The Lord traces for each of us a particular path that is unique and never before seen. Whereas people tend to take refuge in already fixed frameworks, God always invites us to follow a path that is personal to us. And, by the way, he sees much farther than us! So, learning to listen to God runs no risk of cutting us off from ourselves but, on the contrary, preserves us from falling into stereotyped models.

This discernment was at work in Pier Giorgio. No doubt, it was difficult for him because he was being led down a particular path. He would not do the same as his sister who had just got married. He would do otherwise, and it would be truly him. Pier Giorgio could have entered into the race to be married, with the young people of his age, but he discovered that the Lord wanted a different timeframe: If I cannot get married in the present situation, perhaps this has a meaning. I don't get it just now, but later I will understand. His sudden death at the age of twenty-four undoubtedly gives us the key: He had already given his life away.

In fact, Pier Giorgio acted with surprising maturity. Such maturity means accepting not to live for oneself but for others. It enabled him, despite his tribulations, to bear witness again to his love for the people in his life: *". . . I can only thank God every moment for having given me parents, teachers, and all my friends, who have all set me on the royal road of the Faith"* (March 6, 1925).

Discussion Questions

How do I share my feelings with others? Do I hold too much back from them or overshare?

Do I create the space for others to share their feelings with me?

St. Catherine of Siena said that God is "madly in love" with us. What does the experience of falling in love teach us about God?

If I (want to) marry someone, does it matter what my family thinks?

6

Have I Lost the Faith?

Why should I be sad? Why should I suffer . . . ?
Have I perhaps lost the Faith? No, thank God,
my faith is still strong enough. So, let's reinforce
it, strengthen it again, this faith which is the
only Joy that can satisfy us in this world. . . . It
can serve us as a guide and direction our whole
life long and so be a real project for us. Faith can
be, with the grace of God, the goal toward which
my soul tends. Hence, at first, we are terrified
because this project is beautiful but hard, full
of thorns and few roses; but we place our trust
in Divine Providence and in its mercy. . . . For
the one who believes, the adversities of life are
no reason to be despondent. (March 6, 1925)

*W*hen everything was capsizing, Pier
Giorgio clung to his faith, that solid
link with God. He loved talking about faith and
passing it on. But faith has a surprising quality
to it: Paradoxically, it is stable and profoundly

fragile. Indeed, it is anchored in the history of the Church. It is confessed in the same Creed by millions of people. It flourishes through the love of almighty God. And yet, it rests in hearts that are weak and is rooted in the frail and unstable consent of human beings.

In Pier Giorgio, faith became a source of strength when it was not the only virtue he had. Thus, two other virtues are added to faith, especially given by God to bring us closer to him: hope and charity. They adorn the letters of St. Paul and also those of Pier Giorgio. These three theological virtues support each other, forming a well-anchored vessel that endures the storm. The boat represents charity, which sustains our whole life; the anchor, hope, which gives us assurance (cf. Heb 6:19); and faith, the rope that links the two. No matter how rough the sea gets, the boat, tied to its anchor, will avoid even the most dangerous rocks.

During our life on earth, we are caught in this stormy sea. We therefore need faith, tied to hope in the next life, and bound to charity: *"Faith is certainly our only anchor of salvation,"* insisted Pier Giorgio, *"and we have to cling to it firmly. Without it, what would become of our whole life?"* (January 29, 1925). In eternal life, the boat will ride the waves without fear. Faith and hope will no longer be necessary. But charity, for its part, will never pass away. Yes, *"what would faith be, if we didn't clothe it in charity,"* wondered Pier Giorgio (LFC 41).

This is also what St. Paul tells us again: "So faith, hope, love abide, these three; but the greatest of these is love" (1 Cor 13:13). In God, on the Last Day, love will embrace all.

While we're waiting, on this earth, faith remains essential. It binds humanity to God. It binds human hope to that charity which is God. The rope of faith is twined from what we have received from the Church and from our encounters with the Lord. God gives us the first thread, then we twine it with him. This thread never breaks, but it can be stretched to the point where we lose sight of the anchor. It's to this bond that Pier Giorgio clung tight when everything seemed to wobble:

> *There remains, however, a bond which one hopes will, by the grace of God, bind together in this world and the next all the Shady Characters. This sacred bond is the Faith, the only strong bond, the only solid ground, without which nothing can be undertaken. And this Faith, received in holy Baptism, which made us companions on some lovely alpine hikes, will accompany us, we hope, right until the last day of our earthly voyage. May it serve as a bond to spiritually cement, by means of prayer, all the Shady Characters dispersed throughout the world.* (August 11, 1924)

Pier Giorgio experienced periods of deep hopelessness when he saw the political developments in his country and the suffering that was everywhere: *"Today, as I'm writing to you, I am so sad and I need to write to you who, like me, put your trust in the great Goodness of the Lord. I'm not doing it to relieve my heart, which, despite being torn apart, resigns itself only in virtue of that Faith which I learned as a child and which I've fortified through contact with all my friends"* (20 August 1923). Life sometimes seemed to him to have lost its meaning: *"Every day I get more and more sick of things. If I didn't have the certainty that my Faith is Divine, I would certainly abandon myself to doing some stupid things"* (November 16, 1923). And indeed, what meaning can life have when it cuts itself off from its Creator and Savior?

When in total darkness, Pier Giorgio clung to faith, at least so he would not get completely lost. Not to get lost—this core instinct, which might seem quite primitive, enabled him to get back on the Lord's path. When he thought he was drowning, he noticed that the ship of God's love was still carrying him, despite it being buffeted by the waves. When the boat goes off course, Pier Giorgio would take up the words of St. Augustine: "Let me listen to Truth, the Light of my heart, and not to the voices which I heard in the days of my darkness. I deserted truth for worldly things and the night closed over me, but even then, even in my darkness, I continued to love you, O Truth. I wandered away, but I remembered you" (*Confessions* XII, 10).

It only takes a simple act of remembering, and there you have the perseverance of Pier Giorgio. His holiness certainly does not mean he was perfect but refers to this steadfastness: "For in this hope we were saved. Now hope that is seen is not hope. For who hopes for what he sees? But if we hope for what we do not see, we wait for it with patience" (Rom 8:24-25).

In the midst of tumults, Pier Giorgio's vessel keeps on course by the lighthouse which is the cross of Christ. This cross comes at the end of a very dark path but henceforth shines with the light of the Risen One. A Christian has to be prepared to say with St. Paul: "I decided to know nothing among you except Jesus Christ and him crucified" (1 Cor 2:2). Being ready to follow Christ in sorrows and struggles, not just in moments of peace and rest—that's how far Pier Giorgio's faith went. *"Pain without Faith is intolerable, whereas when it is fueled by the torch of the Faith it becomes something beautiful because it tempers our soul for combat. Today, while I have to fight, I can only thank God who wanted in His Infinite Mercy to grant my heart this pain, so that I might return by way of the sharpest thorns to a life that is more interior, more spiritual"* (29 January 1925). Pier Giorgio did not believe God was the source of the evil striking us. But he recognized that all the difficulties we face in our human life are also a path toward God. They only made sense to him because they enabled him to find Jesus.

Faced with doubt, Pier Giorgio had the same confidence as St. Paul: Yes, Lord, your grace is sufficient for me, for your power is made perfect in weakness, for when I am weak, then I am strong (cf. 2 Cor 12:9-10).

Discussion Questions

St. John Henry Newman said that a thousand difficulties do not add up to a single doubt. What are my difficulties with the Faith? Do my difficulties understanding the Faith feel like I'm doubting that the Faith is true?

What aspects of my faith are most vulnerable?

Who are the believers who most inspire me?

Should we have faith in people as well as faith in God? Why or why not?

7

Sitting Exams

I'm writing to you in pencil because I have two fountain pens in front of me which (alas) are empty. . . . I came to Turin with the intention of "stepping on the gas" and seriously studying, otherwise I'll never take this exam, which is getting tiresome the more it's delayed. But to put these intentions into action, one needs an iron will, which unfortunately I do not have; on the contrary, alas, I have a will that is unfortunately accustomed to giving up. So, I need prayers because it's with them, and through them alone, that I will be able to get from God the Grace to strengthen my will, and thus to bring to a safe haven the ship which is currently about to sink under the last stormy waves of my student life. Ruit hora [time marches on] *and so I have to study. Ah, if only I could take this exam within a month, I'd be happy!* (April 17, 1925)

*I*f there's something weighing down Pier Giorgio, it's definitely his studies. Not that he doesn't like them. But to remain sitting at his desk demands an iron will. The first lines of this letter speak volumes about his supercharged, and somewhat disorganized, timetable. That day, he couldn't even muster the courage to fill his two pens with ink! And I admit I find this very reassuring. . . . How many mornings saw Pier Giorgio leave home in a rush as his mother called after him, "Shave yourself!" . . . only for him to arrive late at the university.

His family expected a lot from him when he was not naturally gifted in his studies. Shouldn't he be reaching the standards set by his father— the journalist, ambassador, and senator? Well! Pier Giorgio had made his choice: *"I will be a mining engineer so as to be able to keep devoting myself to Christ through the miners"* (SIC 123). He would do so as an *exemplary* layman. And Giorgio knew well that "exemplary" does not mean "perfect." It's rather about recognizing that one cannot do everything, and yet daring to go right to the end. He was determined to get there, not for his own sake, but for others'.

So he chose his future work with the needs of others in mind: *"I want to be able, in whatever ways possible, to help all the people of my country,"* he confided, *"and I will be better able to do that by remaining in the lay state rather than becoming a priest, because, among us, the priests have no contact with the people. A mining engineer, by giving a good example, can have a more effective impact"* (LFJ 101). His very concrete idea of our Christian mission is striking. If he gave up the idea of becoming a priest, it was only because he was afraid it would prevent him from being among the workers.

By taking part in the student group *Cesare Balbo*—named after an Italian statesman born in Turin in the nineteenth century—Pier Giorgio followed in the footsteps of the movement's founder, opening a dialogue with the contemporary world through cultural, social, and political activity. For him, the university was the best place to carry out this dialogue with his contemporaries. That's where he carried out his daily tasks and engaged with the various currents of thought—and the debates were heated in that period troubled by the beginnings of Fascism. Pier Giorgio was the last to think in tribal terms. Spontaneously, he developed bonds of friendship with the students who did not share his faith. The face of Christ could be seen in these brotherly relations where the Gospel animates, in a more or less hidden way, one of Christ's members. While this student didn't close himself off, neither did he let himself get carried away by all the many currents of thought. He kept a sure hold on the Lord who says to us, "Behold, I make all things new" (Rev 21:5). So, Pier Giorgio was not afraid of novelty. But there's only true renewal when it is animated by the Gospel. To study is to accept that what is new should burst forth in our life every day. In this sense, all study is an act of contemplation that leads us to a new and better vision of the reality which surrounds us.

In this desire to educate himself, Pier Giorgio also drew on *The Dialogue* of St. Catherine of Siena. It was Catherine who, by "loving, [sought] to pursue truth and clothe herself in it," and so heard the Lord say: "Open your mind's eye and look within me, and you will see the dignity and beauty of my reasoning creature" (*Dialogue* 1). God has created us as rational creatures so that we might seek him, that we might desire to know him more and more. To know him, the All-loving, is already to love him.

Pier Giorgio lived in a difficult period when people wondered how to reconcile faith and culture, or the secular state and the Church. He was also faced with the delicate question of the Church's dialogue with an ever-changing world. This dialogue creates a tension that is sometimes worrying because it is destabilizing. Pier Giorgio could have wished to slacken it for his own comfort. But in reality, a Christian is invited to live in this tension, which turns us toward a world that we cannot allow to be constructed without God. It is therefore essential to educate oneself: *"Unfortunately, the students hardly responded to the generous appeal of the Federation, thus showing that they were not conscious of the exalted mission entrusted to them by Divine Providence.*

And so much more in this grave moment which our country is going through, we Catholics, and especially we students, have a grave duty to fulfill: to educate ourselves" (October 30, 1922).

Pier Giorgio has to fight to keep his will firm. How to persevere in his studies which cost him so much? Might we not be ready to admit, with him, *"I have a will that is unfortunately accustomed to giving up"*? Willing is not innate; it must be educated and clothed with the will of God. We are definitely not born saints! Pier Giorgio worked to turn his will toward others. Although he fearlessly admitted his weakness to a friend, he knew where to find the strength to fortify his wobbly will—in prayer. *"I entrust myself to your prayers, but here the studies are not going as I would wish. Too many distractions: I have to make an enormous effort of will to be able to concentrate"* (August 17, 1924). He was wounded by others' lack of confidence in him and his fear of not succeeding. And success was indeed not always the outcome: *"My dear friend, I am writing to tell you the bad news that I have withdrawn from the Thermal Engineering exam. I am not looking for excuses, because I lay the blame mostly on my laziness: but just wait, I'll have to make up for it this summer."* This maturity, nevertheless, did not manage to cover his feeling of failure, as he concluded, *"This year, I've achieved nothing"* (July 22, 1923).

When studying becomes dry or an exam is approaching, the prayer of St. Thomas Aquinas is always within our reach: "Ineffable Creator, you are the true source of light and wisdom. Deign to shed your clarity on the darkness of my understanding. Dispel from me the shades of sin and ignorance. Give me keenness to understand, memory to retain, method and ease to learn, lucidity to interpret, and an abundant grace to speak. Help the beginning of my work, direct its progress, crown its ending. You who are true God and true man, who live and reign, world without end. Amen."

Discussion Questions

Do I empathize with Pier Giorgio's struggles as a student?

Do I (or did I) enjoy school or college?

Where in my life do I struggle?

How do I react when I fail a test?

Do I love God with all my mind (see Mt 22:37)?

8

In Word and in Deed

I am extremely pleased that you want to be part of the great family of St. Dominic, where, as Dante says, "ben s'impingua se non si vaneggia" [there is good fattening unless one goes astray]. *The duties are very minimal, for otherwise, you see, I could not belong to an Order which required a lot. When the Saint instituted the Third Order* [Lay Dominicans], *he instituted it as a militia to fight against the heretics, and so in those days there were very strict rules—one followed more or less the ancient rule of the First Order* [Dominican friars]; *but now it has been transformed, there is no longer any trace of the strict obligations. . . . I hope you will receive the habit in the magnificent church in Turin, and then I will be at your side to give you the fraternal greeting. And so, you who are already attached to me by the bonds of fraternity by the Blood of Our Lord Jesus Christ, will be doubly so when we will have St. Dominic in common as our Father.* (August 31, 1923)

*P*ier Giorgio was a lover of Dante. He knew whole passages, which he would recite out loud in his deep voice: "I was of the lambs of the holy flock that Dominic leads on the path where *there is good fattening if they do not stray*" (*Paradiso* X, 94–6). This little phrase, full of humor, caught Pier Giorgio's attention, and he cited it when talking to a friend about his joining the Dominicans. He discovered life with St. Dominic, in the Order of Preachers, where one can be enriched spiritually— "good fattening" in the virtues—in the green pastures with Christ, the Good Shepherd.

I met Pier Giorgio long before I thought of becoming a Dominican friar. And it was by chance, as a young novice, that I realized that he had been a Lay Dominican and that we were roughly the same age. So I found a brother in him. And a demanding example too! As Dominican brothers, we are preachers . . . often too much in word, and too little in deed. Pier Giorgio recalls us to that equilibrium between actions and words, which does not limit preaching to a few witty remarks on a Sunday. He presses us to act as a complete person and not as a superficial preacher.

Pier Giorgio's first steps in discovering Dominican life were as a kind of bodyguard. . . . Being a strapping man, rather well-built, he offered to accompany the Dominican priest, Filippo Robotti, on his visits to those left behind by society in the slums of Turin—disreputable places, where it was not advisable to walk alone. But wasn't it precisely those places that needed to be visited? No problem; Giorgio was up to it. Absolutely! Somewhat reckless, he didn't hesitate for a second. Father Robotti testified: "In his life, the apostolate went as far as heroism. He quit his family, so to speak, where he could have found every opportunity and the satisfaction of every pleasure, in order to train himself in the hard school of life to develop a strong soul, capable of constancy, energy, courage and sacrifice—capable, in short, of all that is beautiful and noble" (LFC 82). He found among the Dominicans a life of study and contemplation that dares to go out to meet the world, where seeds of Truth can grow. Walking in the footsteps of Christ, this is a mystery wonderfully summarized in the Gospel of John: "They are not of the world, even as I am not of the world. Sanctify them in the truth; your word is truth. As you sent me into the world, so I have sent them into the world" (Jn 17:16-18). A lover of the truth and of reason—a bit crazy, too—one who went as far as the folly of the Cross: "Far be it from me to glory except in the cross of our Lord Jesus Christ, by which the world has been crucified to me, and I to the world" (Gal 6:14). He didn't try to protect himself from the world, but to love it intensely, just as it was. Thus grew his desire to go as far as the frontiers, to see and take what is good, and to leave what is bitter.

In taking the name of Brother Jerome, in honor of Savonarola, Pier Giorgio was boldly following in the footsteps of that colorful and controversial Dominican who was burned at the stake at the end of the fifteenth century. Indeed, Pier Giorgio was a maximalist, and this was what he loved about the Florentine preacher: *"May I one day imitate him in his courage and virtue"* (LFJ 125). He wished to have the courage to proclaim the Gospel and to get things moving when they seemed terribly static and established; to be alive, capable of brave and clear decisions; to be tempered, insofar as he would be sometimes hot, sometimes cold, but never lukewarm; to go as far as to accept the great otherness of God's love, rather than some intermediate compromise; and above all, to beware a sterile and indecisive posture: the *meh* or the *maybe*, which blight our lives. And so, may the Lord not be able to say to us: "I know your works: You are neither cold nor hot. Would that you were cold or hot! So, because you are lukewarm, and neither cold nor hot, I will spew you out of my mouth" (Rev 3:15-16).

Nevertheless, Pier Giorgio was not the utopian Savonarola whom he had taken as a role model. Far from being the rabble-rouser, he was rather the unassuming brother whose deeds, drawing from charity, spoke louder than words. If the Book of Revelation adopts fairly strong language—God vomits up those who are lukewarm—it is more to wake us up, than to scare us. For Giorgio made himself a bearer of that beautiful conviction which St. Thomas Aquinas had strongly emphasized: Human beings are "capable of God." Each of us is made for God, and our true joy is to see God. Pier Giorgio was not a theologian, even if he trained himself spiritually and was an avid reader of St. Thomas and St. Augustine. Motivated also by the letters of the Apostle Paul, he was a seeker of the truth. And so, he did not seek to shine but to illuminate. "For even as it is better to enlighten than merely to shine, so is it better to give to others the fruits of one's contemplation than merely to contemplate" (*Summa* IIa–IIae, q. 188, a. 6).

The prologue to the Rule of St. Augustine, which Pier Giorgio adopted as a Lay Dominican, exhorts us in these words: "Above all, dearest brothers, let us love God, let us love our neighbor: these are the most important commandments given to us." And St. Augustine goes on: "In the very first place, why have you come together if not to live together in unanimity, with one heart and one soul in God. Do not say, 'this is mine,' but that everything for you will be held in common." Without being a friar, as a layman, Pier Giorgio makes this standard his own: "It is rare that people who benefit from material advantages decide to live a life radically opposite to that which their means allow, by seeking poverty and extreme humility" (LFC 111). Finally, Pier Giorgio became a bearer of the mercy of God, of his inexhaustible love for each and every person. That's the spirit of a missionary. He desired to walk with the Church, the People of God, in the confidence that every person has a role to play so that the Church might be the beautiful Bride, dressed and ready for her divine husband—not late to the party or dragging her heels. On many points, Pier Giorgio was a forerunner of that universal call to holiness, which the Second Vatican Council reiterated so strongly. One of his friends captured this well: "What he did, no one else was doing" (LCF 113). That is how we recognize the greatest saints.

Discussion Questions

Do I make resolutions and stick to them?

How do I contribute to the mission of the Church?

If I'm not a member of a spiritual family or order, which one(s) do I find attractive, and why?

9

The Interior Man

The Faith given to me at Baptism speaks to me with a sure voice: "On your own, you will do nothing, but if you take God as the center of all your actions, then you will arrive at the goal." And that is precisely what I want to be able to do, taking as a maxim this saying of St. Augustine: "Lord, my heart is restless until it rests in you." (January 15, 1925)

"*F*racassati!" his friends sometimes shout at him, using a funny nickname that combines his name with the *fracasso*—crash or din—of his outgoing personality. Although Pier Giorgio was noisy because he was so vivacious, humility was also one of the most characteristic signs of his sanctity. He loved to say that *"the true good must be done as if inadvertently, little by little, every day, in a familiar way"* (LFC 78). Hence, his outward actions were seasoned with closeness and discretion.

And if he liked to help others by acting with confidentiality, it was because the Lord was subtly feeding his interior man. He did not put himself at the center but left that place to God: "O Lord, my heart is not proud nor haughty my eyes. I have not gone after things too great nor marvels beyond me. Truly I have set my soul in silence and peace. A weaned child on its mother's breast, even so is my soul" (Ps 130:1-2).

The interior man is like a little child. At the same time, he is great and free when he recognizes in himself the presence of God. Letting God grow freely within us: Maybe that is the definition of human freedom! If the Lord has a place in our lives, he must be able to spread himself out so that he can display his mercy and his love. There is no question of a limited area of our being, of compartmentalization or division. Everything belongs to God, and everything returns to God. The unity of our life comes through the generous expansion of the Kingdom of God in our hearts. By placing ourselves under his watch, under his hand, we experience the greatness of our freedom. And little by little, the interior person gets more in tune with the guest living in them. Pope St. John Paul II, during the beatification of Pier Giorgio, presented him with these simple words: "Behold the interior man" (LFJ 6). And the Pope continued: "All his life seems to summarize the words of Christ which we find in the Gospel of John: 'If a man loves me, he will keep my word, and my Father will love him, and we will come to him and make our home with him' " (Jn 14:23).

When we hear these words, how can we not think of the one who was the "house" of the Lord *par excellence*? Mary—she who welcomed the Word made flesh in her womb. Giorgio loved to meditate on the Annunciation, the first mystery of the Rosary, when the Virgin received the word from the angel. The welcome offered by this humble handmaid is not transient, since what she had the grace to receive transformed her inwardly. She made herself totally available, without any tension or fear. She became the very model of the interior woman. This is what led St. Luke to say these profound words, which themselves deserve to be pondered: "His mother kept all these things in her heart" (Lk 2:51). In her heart of hearts, Mary treasured all the events of our salvation. How much did she understand? Perhaps not all that much. And yet, she received and she retained. And this, too, is how she bore God within her.

Like Mary, Pier Giorgio knew himself to be filled with grace. Had he not received grace upon grace? But how difficult it is in practice to abandon oneself to grace, to let it bloom in us! Such a welcome requires humility and, at the same time, makes humility grow. Giorgio

had the humility to cry to God in his pain
and weakness:

> *Every passing day, I am increasingly convinced
> of how ugly the world is, how much wretchedness
> rules there, and how good people unfortunately
> suffer while we, who have been granted so many
> graces by God, have alas! so poorly responded.
> A horrible realization which torments my mind
> now and then while I'm studying: I wonder if I
> will continue to seek to follow the right path, if
> I will have the fortune to persevere right to the
> end?* (January 15, 1925)

Mary, too, standing at the foot of the Cross,
was a model of perseverance for Pier Giorgio.
She remained there where everyone had abandoned Jesus. And while she was losing her only
son, she was becoming a mother all the more.
She held fast at the summit of Golgotha because
her house had been built upon the rock. The
storms that broke upon her did not shake her.
In this wasteland, would her inner light be
snuffed out?

To be an interior woman or man requires
us to build a home for God within us. But the
tempest comes to blow away the sand of our all
too human foundations, and the unexpected
events that bring us joy or pain rattle our
fragile supports. Pier Giorgio saw the storm
break upon him: *"In any case, I will face up to these*

challenges, hopefully by preparing myself in prayer and in the hope of one day moving on to a better life" (29 July 1924). It would have been a catastrophic landslide, had the raging waters not revealed once more the rock on which the house was but partially built. Giorgio's fears and doubts echo that word humanity had been waiting for: "If the Lord does not build the house, in vain do its builders labor" (Ps 126:1). It is the Lord who builds us a house.

Then came the time for the humble servant to rest: "You made us for yourself, and our hearts find no peace until they rest in you" (*Confessions* I, 1). The one who had felt himself under scrutiny changes his fearful words into a free person's hymn of love to their God: "O Lord, you search me and you know me, you know my resting and my rising, you discern my purpose from afar. You mark when I walk or lie down, all my ways lie open to you . . . your hand ever laid upon me" (Ps 138:1-3). What joy! It's in love that the Lord embraces and constrains us.

The interior house has regained its shape —more modest in size, not quite as long, as wide, or as tall, but with greater depth in the foundations. Throughout his life, Pier Giorgio deepened his interior dwelling, adjusting it, little by little, to the measure of God. Despite his own difficulties, he kept an increasingly spacious place in it for his brothers and sisters in need. As he put it: *"Whoever helps the sick is almost always a blessed person, because it is difficult to take on board the pains of others in addition to the thousand needs, the thousand problems and worries of our own"* (LFC 197). At the end of his life, his worries no longer drowned him and, through his attention to others, he found himself blessed.

The joy of one who is interiorly transformed bubbles up mysteriously on the outside: "Your word struck into my heart and from that moment I loved you. Besides this, all about me, heaven and earth and all that they contain proclaim that I should love you . . . " (*Confessions* X, 6). As St. Augustine says, all creation is now rejoicing. Every sense is awakened to receive the love of God: "A light of a certain kind, a voice, a perfume, a food, an embrace; but they are of the kind that I love in my inner self, when my soul is bathed in light that is not bound by space; when it listens to sound that never dies away; when it breathes fragrance that is not borne away on the wind; when it tastes food that is never consumed by the eating; when it clings to an embrace from which it is not severed by fulfillment of desire. This is what I love when I love my God" (*Confessions* X, 6).

Discussion Questions

Do I find it difficult to sit still?

Do I enjoy silence, or find it uncomfortable?

When I face difficult situations, is it more important to act or to be patient? What factors or circumstances might change my response?

What did Mary feel when she saw her son Jesus growing up, preaching and healing, dying, and rising?

10

Charity Sows Peace

*My friends . . . you do not need to hear rehashed
in petty words those things which you have
heard so many times before. But given the grav-
ity of the problem, I do not believe it is useless to
repeat such well-known points. Every one of you
knows that the fundamental basis of our religion
is Charity, without which our whole religion
would collapse. . . . The Catholic faith is based
on true Love and not—as so many other people
would have it for the sake of tranquilizing their
consciences—taking violence as the basis of
the Religion of Christ. With violence, hatred is
sown, and then we harvest the evil fruit of such
a sowing. With charity, Peace is sown among
people: not the peace of the world, but the True
Peace which only Faith in Jesus Christ can give
us to make us brothers and sisters of one another.*
(February 1922)

*O*nly love makes it possible to build true peace. Pier Giorgio was convinced of this. For him, it's not about throwing the question back onto a distant, utopian project. Rather, it is necessary to act in the present moment. That is why he insisted: *"It's important to do good, that's the principal thing. What does it matter if it is a Sunday or not? A neighbor needs us and we have to serve them, whatever the day of the week"* (LFC 196). Doing good, so that peace may grow, is to serve the Lord, who, like a sower, spreads his love upon the earth. From this love sown, peace will germinate. This peace comes from God, for it is nourished by his love, yet it is brought about on earth. "Mercy and faithfulness have met; justice and peace have embraced. Faithfulness shall spring from the earth and justice look down from heaven. The Lord will make us prosper and our earth shall yield its fruit" (Ps 84:11-13).

The peace we want to have around us must first take root in us. We need to let ourselves be pacified by the Lord in our deepest being. Our heart can fall prey to a kind of blaring violence, heckled by contrary forces, and a little bit of silence is enough to reveal the powerful activity that moves us inwardly. Pier Giorgio had within him those passions and emotions, which have to be ordered if they are to bear good fruit. He made an effort to let the Lord calm these passions down and orient them, not toward selfish satisfaction of his own desires but toward the love of neighbor, ceaselessly wanting the good, for where the good no longer thrives, evil takes its place. "Turn aside from evil and do good; seek and strive after peace" (Ps 33:15). In this area, there is no room for compromise: It requires daily vigilance.

The peaceful person, the one who has found the place of interior rest, can become a blessing to those around them. They bear the fruits of peace. Pier Giorgio progressively acquired this disposition, and he avoided making cheap criticisms of others. When sometimes he got carried away, he promptly recognized his wrongs. After an evening's passionate discussion about politics, he confessed: *"I think I even lost my rag and I exaggerated a bit, but in these matters my spirit rejects half-measures"* (January 9, 1924). He, too, knew himself to be a sinner and, while sustained by high ideals, he did not consider himself worthy to judge others. In this way, he showed his great maturity, that of a man who really knew the trials and temptations of those who were just like him. He preferred to carry them in prayer and, by his gentleness and goodness, to lead them toward peace. Violence in language can be more deadly than physical brutality. Charity flowed, then, through the words which came from his human heart, purified in love.

For Pier Giorgio, charity went out to every person, whatever their origin or religion. Charity is the preeminently *Catholic*—i.e., universal—

virtue because it leaves no one out: *"Never let any human being be abandoned"* (LFC 196). Pier Giorgio did not close the door to a friend who was drifting away from the Faith, unlike several of his acquaintances who were closed off by their inflexibility. He was friendly with everyone, without distinction of social class. That was why he did not try to rally the poor against the rich. Conscious of what he had received, he freely gave things away—money, yes, but especially the vigor of his youthfulness, the peace of his kind consideration, the simplicity of his deeds. Such charity toward everyone fosters the emergence of justice. And justice is the condition of that peace, which, for Pier Giorgio, is necessarily built on human equality. He thought of it firstly as something to be received from God: *"When we all accept the words and the teaching of Christ, we will be able to say that we are equals and every difference between people will be abolished"* (LFC 70). The equality to which we aspire comes from God, who transforms our hearts to welcome the "other" as a brother or sister.

But it would be too simple to stop there! Equality is also built in a more concrete way: *"How could anyone explain the admirable resignation of so many poor creatures who fight with life and so often die in the breach, if it were not for the certainty of the Justice of God"* (January 15, 1925). Yes, poverty is scandalous. Yes, the justice of God will reveal what is hidden. Yes, the Lord will save the unhappy person who has no other help. Pier Giorgio had the clarity of one who wanted to see with God's eyes. And every possession that was not turned to the good appeared to him as something violent—that is, violence toward others, but primarily toward the one who is self-imprisoned by it. "Then do not fear when a man grows rich, when the glory of his house increases. He takes nothing with him when he dies, his glory does not follow him below. Though he flattered himself while he lived: 'Men will praise me for all my success,' yet he will go to join his fathers, and will never see the light any more. In his riches, man lacks wisdom; he is like the beasts that are destroyed" (Ps 49:17-21).

Clarity of vision puts everything in its right place. Even the most insignificant details are clarified by charity. Pier Giorgio arrived one day at the Popular Party, wearing an old hat that was pretty hideous. A young lady could not resist commenting: "Oh! Frassati, you could have changed your hat," to which he replied, *"Miss, if you had been with me in the hovel where I was just a moment ago, you would understand that it isn't worth changing one's hat. With the money that it costs, one could do some good"* (LFC 107). Lord, come to change our hearts, which are hiding behind the blindness of our eyes. Awaken our slumbering senses and turn us into peacemakers so that we might say with St. Augustine: "You called me; you cried aloud to me; you broke my barrier of deafness. You shone upon me; your radiance enveloped me; you put my blindness to flight. You shed your fragrance about me; I drew breath and now I gasp for your sweet odor. I tasted you, and now I hunger and thirst for you. You touched me, and I am inflamed with love of your peace" (*Confessions* X, 27).

Discussion Questions

Do I take an interest in social and political questions?

How do I engage with people who disagree with me?

What hidden forms of violence can I learn to unmask, in society or in my personal life?

11

Beyond the Frontiers

In these days, when all evil is showing itself in its most nauseating aspects, I carry on while thinking of the days we passed together. I remember the first elections in the postwar period, the coming of Fascism, and now I also remember with joy that we were never in favor of Fascism, not even for an instant in our past life, but we have always fought against this scourge of Italy. . . . We may call ourselves the fortunate ones, who, through the Goodness of God, have set out on a road which, although we sometimes left it momentarily, we immediately returned to. This very different road does not give us the delights of the world, which anyway can only be bought at the price of one's conscience. Certainly, if we continue right to the end of the road laid out for us by the teachings of Our Lord Jesus Christ, it will lead us to the triumph of the next life. (June 21, 1924)

*P*ier Giorgio was thirteen years old when the First World War broke out. That's why the urgent need for peace is like a refrain in many letters from his teenage years. Later, in 1921, when his father was appointed ambassador to Berlin, he saw for the first time the faces of the losers from the last war. He was moved by the suffering and poverty of the German people, and he took the side of the losers. The postwar period and the crippling terms of the Treaty of Versailles deeply saddened the young man. How could this unjust "justice" lead to peace? In the end, he realized that the only justice that can lead to peace is not human justice, but God's, for whom forgiveness is the highest act of love. Pier Giorgio was prophetic when he wrote to German students: *"True Peace is more the fruit of Christian love of neighbor than of justice"* [Pope Pius XI]. *But they are preparing new wars in the future for all humanity. Modern society is sinking in the sufferings of human passions and is distancing itself from every ideal of love and of peace"* (January 12, 1923).

Peace depends on giving without expectation of return, something that only the Lord can do perfectly. When he was born, the heavens reverberated with the peace that Jesus brought by making himself a little infant: "peace on earth to people of [God's] goodwill" (cf. Lk 2:14). And he gave his life for peace right to the end: By the death of this just man on the cross, he restored justice forever. The *lex talionis*, the law of exact retaliation, the ancient "eye for an eye, tooth for a tooth," has been surpassed and brought to a new perfection. The spiral of hatred is broken upon the unimaginable love of God offered to all; in his body on the cross, he killed hostility, St. Paul explains (cf. Eph 2:16). A new law of love is now possible for us: "Love one another, even as I have loved you" (Jn 13:34). God so loved us that he gave his own life for us. Christ goes further, in giving us an unprecedented commandment: "Love your enemies" (Mt 5:44). Christ does not ask us to love the evil done to us, but to find what is loveable in our enemies. It's a short saying but one of the most powerful of all the teachings of Jesus.

Pier Giorgio took that commandment as his rule of conduct. He kept overcoming barriers by taking the side of the Germans when they were held in disgrace by all of Europe, and the side of the poor who were abandoned by the well-off in the Popular Party once the Fascists took power. At the heart of the Gospel, he heard these words: "You are all brethren" (Mt 23:8):

> *In these tragic and painful moments, when your country is trodden down by the feet of foreigners, when your rival turns into an enemy of your country and occupies your homes, we Catholic students are sending you the expression of our fraternal love. We do not have the ability to change this sad situation, but we feel in us all*

the strength of our Christian love which makes
us brothers and sisters beyond the frontiers of all
the nations. (January 12, 1923)

Giorgio knew that we are all brothers and sisters because we have God as our common Father. Recognizing God in the person of our brother or sister allows us to love him or her, no matter what bad things they might have done.

So, his involvement in the city should not be understood only in terms of its political aspect. For Pier Giorgio, the social crisis was only the visible tip of a deeper and more widespread religious crisis—the absence of God and ideologies of atheism. Refusing to be silenced was his first step toward action. *"I understand that words make little difference, but at least we will make them understand that the Catholic students do not agree with the politics of the Italian government, and that they are indignant at the European politics which will lead all the nations to destruction"* (January 10, 1923). But how hard it was to let peace be heard when the hearts around him were closed! In his heart of hearts, Giorgio heard the Apostle's resounding appeal: "Do not be conformed to this world but be transformed by the renewal of your mind, that you may prove what is the will of God, what is good and acceptable and perfect" (Rom 12:2).

Building peace in us and around us, that's the urgent challenge for every Christian. And this is not beyond our reach: The Gospel is lived in a radius of one meter around us. No need to go looking for distant conflict zones. Pier Giorgio was a peacemaker in his family, broken by all its mindless quarrels, as he was also among the poorest of the poor who were there at his gate.

Even the smallest deed of goodwill, the most insignificant good, becomes necessary when evil is on the prowl. Giorgio was one of those people who, without special qualifications, made himself an ambassador for peace. And there was no time to lose:

> *As Catholics, you and we have to bring the breath of goodness which alone is born of faith in Christ. Brothers and sisters, in these new trials and terrible torments, know that the great Christian family is praying for you. Act in such a way that your sufferings and your combats may be lightened for you. Just as the peace of the world cannot return without God, you who are people of goodwill should at least keep in your hearts the One in the cave* [at Bethlehem] *who was announced by Angels—the Savior of Humanity.* (January 12, 1923)

Against all this violence, he was no less resolved to fight and die for Christ. As the war carted off its piles of the dead, Pier Giorgio was pierced to the heart. He asked Natalina, the chambermaid, who had lost her brother in the war, *"Wouldn't you give your life to make the war stop?"* "Certainly not I," she replied, "I am young, and my life is worth more than that of the soldiers." So, Giorgio retorted forcefully: *"Well, as for me, I am ready to give my life, even today"* (LFJ 61).

Discussion Questions

What other states or countries have I travelled to?

Am I in close contact with people beyond my local community?

As well as looking after local needs, how can I reach out to those in dire need beyond the horizon?

12

Right Living

I would like to go forward on the right path, but at every step I stumble and fall. For this reason, I exhort you to pray as much as you can for me, so that I may arrive, on the day willed by Divine Providence, at the end of this wearisome but straight path. These days, in the meantime, I am alternating dry studies with the marvelous reading of St. Augustine. My spirit has never before experienced in such a strong way a delight which has no end. For through these powerful Confessions *one tastes a little of that joy which will be reserved for those who die under the Sign of the Cross. Today I lament bitterly that I have so often wasted my time and have waited until I am so old to taste such pure joys.* (December 20, 1924)

*P*ier Giorgio was only twenty-three years old when he wrote those lines, with just a few months left to live. Did he already have a feeling his pilgrimage on earth was coming to an end? In any case, he tasted the joy of one who resumes the journey after too long a break and gets back to walking in the footsteps of Christ. Isn't the Christian precisely the one who sees themselves as a pilgrim, even in their own home? God invites us to keep going along the road, without ever thinking we have arrived and, if possible, to walk along the straight path.

This path is not determined by markers on the sides that would fix its limits. It's more a matter of having someone walking alongside us, whether we are going forward or falling or stopping. The straight path is not necessarily the one that leads in a straight line to the destination, but the path where we are constantly making progress in the company of him who gave his life for us. That's how we, in turn, experience our own road to Emmaus: "While they were talking and discussing together, Jesus himself drew near and went with them" (Lk 24:15). Jesus walks with us on our earthly pilgrimage and his simple presence makes it a straight path, despite the undergrowth and the falls. For he is not only a pilgrim: He is also the Way, the pilgrimage made flesh.

It's not a single path. As someone who liked to climb mountains, Pier Giorgio knew this well. Many paths exist, and still more. . . . Some are direct and easy; others are perilous and long but sometimes more beautiful. They are beautiful

in virtue of the goal they have set themselves.
They are beautiful in the landscapes they present to the eye. But they are true and profoundly
good when they provide a place of encounter.
When Pier Giorgio was alone, that encounter
was certainly that of the young man with his
Lord. When it was a group outing, it was an
encounter with a brother or sister.

Pier Giorgio had to wrestle with his emotions and did not achieve such an apparently
natural goodness without numerous combats
first: "How shall the young remain sinless? By
obeying your word. I have sought you with all
my heart; let me not stray from your commands"
(Ps 118:9-10). The Lord does not choose the
equipped but he equips those he chooses. So, on
the way of holiness, it's not about following a
predefined itinerary. On the contrary, our walking teaches us to be who we are—to be nothing
other than who we are.

That's why this path is never laid out in
advance. God leads us on the road, but also,
mysteriously, lets himself be led. He sets out to
find us whenever we stray far from him and walk
in our own ways. God accepts being "surprised"
by human beings because he has the most beautiful plans for us: The Lord loves for human beings
to journey with him along the many ways that
lead to him. The whole story of the Bible shows
us a God who follows the ups and downs of our
human lives. If our plans, established without

reference to him, are but those of an instant, God accepts the overturning of his own plans in order to give us life. As the saying goes, "God writes straight with crooked lines."

To make progress on the way, we have to allow ourselves to stumble and not refuse to be picked up afterward. It's also about accepting that we are walking with others and need to be a support to them:

> *Certainly, Divine Providence in Its Wonderful Plans so often makes use of us pathetic twigs to work for the Good, and we so often do not want to know, or even dare to deny, His Existence. But we, Thanks be to God, have the Faith. When we find ourselves in the presence of such beautiful souls, certainly nourished by the Faith, we cannot but recognize in them a manifest sign of the Existence of God, for such Goodness could not be had without the Grace of God.* (April 10, 1925)

For Pier Giorgio, his walking companions became signs of the Lord's goodness. The trust we place in Jesus, and the trust he shows us, enable us to spring forward toward eternal life: "Not that I have already obtained this or am already perfect; but I press on to make it my own, because Christ Jesus has made me his own. Brethren, I do not consider that I have made it my own; but one thing I do, forgetting

what lies behind and straining forward to what
lies ahead, I press on toward the goal for the
prize of the upward call of God in Christ Jesus"
(Phil 3:12-14).

On the way, people fall, get wounded, and
even die. Pier Giorgio experienced these several
"deaths" which can mark our existence. But he
observed that, in spite of everything, life ceaselessly bursts forth again: *"Death, what does that
word mean? If by 'death' you mean it in the ordinary
sense, then I am still alive, unless my senses are deceiv-
ing me. But if you mean the word in its true essence,
then unfortunately not only am I dead, but already
many times I have risen, alas only to die again"*
(December 20, 1924).

He also knew that our earthly life is com-
pleted by death, and he would be no exception.
He was all the more alive for his awareness of
our human condition, without fear or taboo:

> *Since a person does not know when Death will
> take them, it makes very good sense to prepare
> yourself every day to die that same day. So,
> from now on, I will try each day to make a little
> preparation for death, to avoid finding myself
> unprepared at the hour of death and lament-
> ing the good years of youth, wasted in spiritual
> terms. And you, what will you do? What do
> you think of these resolutions, which I hope
> I can keep by the grace of God?* (July 19, 1923)

Knowing that we will die should not terrify us. On the contrary, this can allow us to stay focused on what really matters. And thus, to live to the full all that is given to us today.

Death can only be faced effectively because we know that it does not have the last word. The *Divine Comedy*, which Pier Giorgio had at his fingertips, reminds us precisely of the goal of our Christian pilgrimage. We need to go right to God, the living center of the world. "I saw a point which radiated a light so keen that the eye on which it burns must close for its piercing power. . . . From that point hang the heavens and all nature" (*Paradiso* XXVIII, 16–18, 41–42). This light is a sun "which first warmed my breast with love" (*Paradiso* III, 1). On the way, the Lord gives us a wonderful promise: "Lo, I am with you always, to the close of the age" (Mt 28:20). So, along this way, love! And show it by your life.

Discussion Questions

Do I know how to forgive myself when I fail?

Am I jealous of others in their vocations or life opportunities?

How do my friends or family support me in leading a Christian life?

How do I cope with thoughts of death or the experience of bereavement?

13

Our Daily Bread

I exhort you with all the strength of my heart to approach as often as you can the Eucharistic Table. Be fed with this Bread of Angels and you will draw from it the strength to fight your internal battles, the battles against the passions and against all adversities. For to those who are fed with the Most Holy Eucharist, Jesus Christ has promised Eternal Life and the Graces necessary to obtain it. (July 29, 1923)

Approaching his adolescent years, Pier Giorgio adopted the habit of receiving Holy Communion every day. It was a priest who suggested it to him, and Giorgio at first found the idea surprising, as he had often heard his parents criticize those "pious little women" who visit the church every day. But his deep desire was stronger and, after several days of insistence, he managed to overcome his mother's opposition. He took this line from the Lord's Prayer and made

it his own: "Give us this day our daily bread."
Henceforth, he received Holy Communion daily.

In the Eucharist, Pier Giorgio received the
Body and Blood of Christ who gave his life for us.
Every other human utterance is enlightened by
this sublime saying: "This is my body." A saying
so simple, yet it contains all the beauty of God
become human: "the Word became flesh and
dwelt among us" (Jn 1:14). A saying of astonishing
power, which changes the bread into the Body of
the Lord. In this action accompanied by a word,
we ceaselessly take part in a new creation. Reality
is transformed, or rather it is fulfilled more perfectly. The bread has never been so nourishing;
it has never been so fully the "living bread"
(Jn 6:48, 51). By the words of Consecration, this
specifically human food becomes highly spiritual
nutrition—"the bread of angels."

In *The Dialogue*, which Pier Giorgio read
at the end of his life, St. Catherine of Siena
learned that "in communion the soul seems
more sweetly bound to God and better knows
his truth. For then the soul is in God and God
in the soul, just as the fish is in the sea and the
sea in the fish" (*Dialogue* 2). Thus, God makes
himself over most intimately to each person—by
becoming their food—while at the same time
offering himself to all.

Pier Giorgio did not receive Communion
without preparing himself spiritually and physi-
cally for the guest he was to welcome. That was

why he scrupulously respected the Eucharistic
fast, eating nothing from midnight to the Mass.
Even in the mountains, he would walk for long
hours on an empty stomach in order to be able to
receive the Body of the Lord upon arrival. Was
that unreasonable? It was the most beautiful and
the most concrete way he found to let his desire
to receive the Lord grow in him. So, around the
age of twelve, his mother started to get worried:
"Every evening . . . he went to Benediction given
in the church of the Capuchins, very close by,
while we were going for a stroll. He left the hotel
without eating anything, without anyone knowing, in order to hear Mass" (LFJ 53). But the
young adolescent had known for a long time that
it was no mere matter of "hearing Mass."

In this way, two tables are featured in the life
of Pier Giorgio: the dining table and the table of
the Eucharist. For him, they were two—very
different—silent meals. At the family table,
Giorgio tended to wall himself up in silence.
Since he could not talk about his faith, he often
kept his mouth shut. He would say grace on his
own before entering the dining room. One day
when he was late for breakfast, his mother commented: "This is so like him . . . his head in the
clouds, he remembers he needs to go to Mass but
not that he has to come to table! He must have
stayed in his bedroom" (LFJ 69).

Little by little, this silence, instead of leading
to unproductive apathy, was filled by his daily

communion with the Body of Christ. Indeed, Pier Giorgio learned in Eucharistic Communion another type of silence, which is dialogue. During the Eucharist, God speaks to our innermost heart. He gives himself, and his word resounds in the heart of a deep silence, in the sanctuary of our soul. In response, from the human heart, these very grateful words of St. Augustine can arise: "Give yourself to me, my God; restore yourself to me. I show you my love, but if it is too little, give me strength to love you more" (*Confessions* XIII, 8). In the Host, we are offered the most beautiful word and the longest silence—the silence of the Passion, when Jesus was faced with insults but "opened not his mouth" (Is 53:7), and the silence of the Resurrection before the empty tomb: "He is not here; for he has risen" (Mt 28:6). Silence is an essential condition for receiving the Lord. Although it is an interior silence, it is difficult to do without an exterior silence. So, Pier Giorgio decided to take time off for silence and retreat, as he wrote to a friend: *"I think I need a little time in silence to receive spiritual things and to do a little spring cleaning"* (April 3, 1925).

The Eucharist gives direction to our whole life. In the life of Pier Giorgio, God made himself present through this sacrament and accompanied him on his way with his brothers and sisters. And yet, this sign of bread indicates simultaneously the full presence and the hiddenness of God. Communion elicits the desire to know the Christ whose Body withdraws even as it gives itself. God does not want to be loved on account of any material advantage he may give. He fills not our treasure chests, but the chests of our hearts. He presents himself to us in the most unassuming way—as a piece of bread. And yet, there he is giving us his very self. That is the astonishing mystery.

In the Eucharist, God presents himself without dazzle, in the humblest form. "He had no form or comeliness that we should look at him, and no beauty that we should desire him" (Is 53:2). Trivial food and yet so rich in promise. This food is received in the home of our heart. It comes to reveal to us our profound unity: The One whom our body receives, the soul welcomes at the same time.

Bread, such a basic foodstuff, revealed to Pier Giorgio the presence of God in the midst of what is most commonplace. Making bread involves a great variety of human activities, including transport and trade. Even what might appear the least spiritual thing to human eyes is invited to bear the presence of God in the world. Trusting in the Eucharist strengthens our trust in everything else, especially in the most common things. By this sacrament, the ordinary becomes extraordinary and the everyday is clothed in the eternity of God.

The grace of such a simple sacrament as the Eucharist renewed the interior life of Pier

Giorgio and his way of seeing the world. One day, one of his friends said of a dilapidated house: "If I were the landlord, I would have this hovel demolished!" Giorgio could not refrain from replying: *"Oh, if only you knew how many lovely people live in these houses that you call hovels!"* (LFJ 52). He knew that the humblest shack could house the heart of a king—that with a piece of bread, God can nourish his people. Pier Giorgio grew to see in hardship and distress, in what is small and humble, the face of the Lord: *"Jesus comes to visit me every day in Communion, and I return the kindness in such a small way by visiting the poor who belong to him"* (LFC 21).

Discussion Questions

Is Sunday Mass an important time in my week? Do I experience it as an obligation or routine or something more life-giving? Why?

Do I fast and prepare spiritually to receive Holy Communion? Is the Eucharist living bread for my journey through the week? What actions nourish me in my faith life?

If God humbled himself to become human, even giving his life on the Cross, how can I humbly give my life to God?

14

Time Is Short

Up to this age I have now reached, I have lived too materialistically, and today I need to fortify my spirit again for future struggles. Because from now on, every day and every hour there will be a new battle to fight and a new victory to win. There needs to be in me a spiritual conversion, and that's why this year I will apply myself to reading St. Thomas Aquinas. Thus absorbed in those marvelous pages, every thought of the world will be put to death and I will live happy days. For they alone give the heart a joy without end, which is not a human but a true joy. (January 29, 1925)

*T*oday Pier Giorgio tumbles down the stairs. He fails to button his collar correctly, and calls out, *"I'm grabbing a cup of coffee and then I'm off to see a sick man at the hospital"* (LFC 195). He hesitates to buy a ticket, but eventually, as he's running late, jumps on board a tram heading

north to the Cottolengo Hospital, behind the
Church of the *Consolata* that is so dear to him.
He has an appointment today with a sick man
. . . with God himself. Tomorrow may be the
same. But "the hour is coming and now is" (Jn
4:23). From now on, every hour matters—the
Kingdom comes today. Pier Giorgio discovered,
through the sick and the dying, that our life must
build itself in the present. Why be forever putting
off the time to finally serve and walk on the way
of the Gospel? Pier Giorgio was convinced that
*"a visit to the Cottolengo would do good to all people.
It would make them understand life's genuine values,
releasing them from appearances and the unconscious
surrender to everyday existence"* (LFC 84).

   To be honest, Pier Giorgio seemed to have as
much trouble with time-management as we do.
He never had enough. And yet, he was master of
his time since he gave it up to God. The path he
gets us to walk is not one of laziness. *"We shouldn't
just get along, but live!"* (February 27, 1925).

   Pier Giorgio was not naturally hyper-
active. He knew how much a human heart can
be sluggish, earthly, and inclined to only gradual
change. There are many reasons to put off an
undertaking or a conversion. This confession,
which he was ready to make himself, he found
already in St. Augustine telling the Lord, " 'Soon,'
'Presently,' 'Let me wait a little longer' " . . . but
he noticed that " 'soon' was not soon and 'a little
longer' grew much longer" (*Confessions* VIII, 5).

Nonetheless, Pier Giorgio found in God the strength to get going: "His charity was not only in his constant giving, but in that inexhaustible strength which always held him ready, today, tomorrow, the next day, to run forth with the same enthusiasm" (LFC 141). He got to his feet, ready to love God and his neighbor, to serve his brothers and sisters, and advanced with determination, never losing sight of Christ. Like a long-distance runner, he never tired of visiting the poor. He was even nicknamed "the boy who always runs." And in order to be immediately helpful, he was willing to use any means available! One day, a friend saw him carting a heavy load and asked him, "Who does that wheelbarrow belong to, and who allowed you to use it?" The reply came simply: *"I don't know; a lady who had seen me with a sack on my shoulder pointed out this means of transport, and so I used it"* (SIC 150). To serve, spontaneously!

For Pier Giorgio, time is short because the Gospel needs to be proclaimed to the world. The Spirit of the Lord "has anointed me to bring good tidings to the afflicted; he has sent me to bind up the broken-hearted, to proclaim liberty to the captives, and the opening of the prison to those who are bound; to proclaim the year of the Lord's favor" (Is 61:1-2). This passage, which Jesus read in the synagogue of Nazareth, marked the beginning of the proclamation of the Gospel. Christ commented simply: "Today

this Scripture has been fulfilled in your hearing"
(Lk 4:21). The Lord asks us to hear this "today"
of the word of God. It is *now* that the word speaks
to us and gives us life. Let us leave tomorrow to
worry about itself (cf. Mt 6:34).

Nonetheless, *"time passes me by terribly fast
. . . the years pass, and one gets old and so one has to
apply a little discernment"* (August 8, 1923). Our
earthly life is short. "Our span is seventy years,
or eighty for those who are strong. And most of
these are emptiness and pain. They pass swiftly
and we are gone" (Ps 89:10). But our faith in
God's promise of eternal life must not, therefore, devalue our present life. Every moment is
infinitely precious and carries with it something
of God's eternity. The Lord gives time all its
weight. Thanks to him, our earthly journey is
no mere trifle.

That is why each of our lives is precious and
must be a struggle for the good. Pier Giorgio is
telling us that time is only short because there
is a battle to be fought. But did not Jesus, meek
and humble of heart, come to bring peace? So
why fight, and against whom? We fight for our
bodily well-being with strength and vigor. Do we
have the same ardor for our spiritual well-being?
Confronted by evil in all its forms, we cannot
close our eyes. We must fight against it, both
within ourselves and around us. Jesus challenges
us: "Do not think that I have come to bring peace
on earth; I have not come to bring peace, but a

sword" (Mt 10:34). This sword does not lead to death. It is there to cut off whatever is harmful to unity and to recover the heart of flesh from underneath its stone casing.

Pier Giorgio's struggle had a goal: "He was a magnificent 'Pauline wrestler,' an authentic contestant, because he always contested by love, never by disgust or by meanness. He fought to build, never to destroy, he wrestled to lift up, never to cast down" (COD 255). Indeed, just like St. Paul, Pier Giorgio equipped himself with a faith full of vitality. "Do you not know that in a race all the runners compete, but only one receives the prize? So run that you may obtain it. Every athlete exercises self-control in all things. They do it to receive a perishable wreath, but we an imperishable. Well, I do not run aimlessly, I do not box as one beating in the air" (1 Cor 9:24-26). Pier Giorgio immersed himself in Paul's Epistles, whom he loved for his audacity and perseverance. *"The struggle is hard, and yet it is necessary to seek to overcome and find our little road to Damascus, to be able to walk along it toward that goal to which we must all arrive. . . . Will I have the strength to arrive?"* (January 29, 1925).

Pier Giorgio's life was cut short by his untimely death, but this did not take him by surprise. He was ready, he was waiting, and he bore his fruit in due season (cf. Ps 1:3). In the end, he could humbly say, "I have fought the good fight, I have finished the race, I have kept the faith" (2 Tim 4:7). With the Lord, he was able to start every day anew.

Discussion Questions

Am I a busy person, and does this give me a sense of self-importance?

When I procrastinate, what do I waste my time doing?

If God only gives me 24 hours in the day, that must be enough. What resources are most limited in my day? Are there ways I can structure my time to be more effective?

Do I make myself available for others, including unexpected encounters? How so?

At the end of my life, what will I most regret having failed to do?

15

The Power of Prayer

Unfortunately, one by one, earthly friendships bring sorrows to our hearts when those we love move away, but I would like us to swear a pact that knows no earthly bounds, no limits in time: union in prayer. (January 15, 1925)

Prayer is the noble supplication which we lift up to the throne of God and is the most effective means to obtain from God the graces we need, and in particular the strength to persevere. (July 29, 1923)

*A*n insistence on prayer punctuates the letters of Pier Giorgio like a refrain: We need *"continual prayer in order to get from God that grace without which our strength fails"* (October 30, 1922). Convinced of the power of prayer for oneself and for others, it saturated his whole day. "Is it true that when you are in your room, you spend a long time in prayer?" a priest questioned him one day.

Faced with a dumbstruck Pier Giorgio, he continued: "I know it, your mother told me. Well, you're
causing her some anxiety; she gets up during the
night." *I have so many prayers to say,"* murmured
Giorgio. "And who is forcing you to say them?"
"No one. I just have to say them" (LFJ 68). Even
the man of the Church seemed not to grasp the
freedom that drove Pier Giorgio to pray. It was
because he felt a deep desire to pray that he loved
to do it so often. It was no duty except one of love.

For him, it was not so much a matter of
"saying your prayers" as spending time in the
company of his Lord, his master and his friend.
Moreover, this intimacy with Jesus did not limit
itself to a few repetitive formulas; when he did
use these, he always went beyond them to find
God himself. This was why he found praying
irresistible, an obligation of love, and the duty
of a friend toward a very dear friend, since, for
him, to pray is above all to love.

"Lord, teach us to pray" (Lk 11:1). Isn't this
perhaps the underlying request in everyone's
prayer life? It can become our first prayer. Very
often we can start there, whether everything
is going well, or our spiritual life is wobbling:
Lord, I don't know. . . . Teach me. By these
simple words, I'm already speaking to God; I
recognize someone in my presence. In admitting
this, I give him back something of myself, something of what is most precious to me and which
sustains me from the bottom of my heart. And

it is from *learning* that prayer is born—learning how to pray, to know oneself, and thus to love.

The life of Pier Giorgio bears witness to a permanent, humble, and faithful apprenticeship. He received from his parents, from his friends and teachers, and from the mountain, too. Thus, he learned how to be always listening to God. By the way, that was the sole and very beautiful reply of King Solomon, when God asked him what he desired: "Give me, Lord, a listening heart" (cf. 1 Kings 3:9). The attentive ear of Pier Giorgio made him a man who listened. This interior disposition was something stable, or rather, something continually renewing itself: "Pray constantly, give thanks in all circumstances" (1 Thess 5:17-18). Prayer takes flesh in the listening heart. Asking for such a heart is the original prayer that leads to all the others.

To that first, seemingly fearful and clumsy, request from the Apostles, Jesus replied with the Our Father: "Father, hallowed be thy name" (Lk 11:2). Christ unites his voice with ours in that trustfulness which makes us sons and daughters of God, whose name of "Father" truly makes us brothers and sisters.

The Our Father, lit up with ten Hail Marys, formed the backdrop of Pier Giorgio's prayer. Indeed, he especially loved the Rosary. He made his own rosary with Job's tears, tough little beads from an amazing plant, which he grew in the garden at Pollone. He loved to pray the Rosary because it is the ultimate prayer of the poor:

There is no need to be literate to pray the Rosary. In it, we meditate on the whole life of Jesus: his infancy, his passion, and his resurrection—the Joyful, Sorrowful, and Glorious Mysteries—the silent mystery, too, of the hidden life of Jesus, which Pier Giorgio imitated in his charitable acts, unbeknownst even to his closest relations.

Truly, the Rosary is the prayer of the poor person who either doesn't dare or doesn't know how to pray anymore. When prayer becomes arid, and God no longer seems to answer, when the attentive ear can no longer discriminate between the noise of the world and the great silence of God, or when there's a dead calm, that's when Pier Giorgio would take his rosary out of his pocket, where he always kept it at hand. And so he would pray to Jesus with Mary.

The Rosary was for him a meditation in motion: He prayed it on the tram or walking or climbing. During the holidays, early in the morning, he would climb to the Marian sanctuary of Oropa, rosary in hand, and still manage to make it home again before the rest of the household rose. *"First let us greet Our Lady, and then we will have a snack,"* he loved to declare before setting out from Oropa (SIC 264). We see his resilient humor when, sliding down suddenly from an ascent and in response to the anxious prayer of one of his teammates, he quipped with a grin: *"Why bother Our Lady about such a little thing?"* (SIC 263).

Yet Mary was a constant support for him, the "fixed goal of the eternal counsel," as Dante calls her (*Paradiso* XXXIII, 3). He also offered his prayers to all the saints. In this communion of heaven and earth, Pier Giorgio loved to pray to St. Francis and St. Dominic, who are so close to Mary, forming "this garland which surrounds with looks of love the fair lady who strengthens thee for heaven" (*Paradiso* X, 91–3).

Prayer is wide, spacious, and beautiful when it is not limited to oneself. It has no appetite for itself but is a communion with God, with our brothers and sisters, and with the world. It risks turning in on itself whenever it turns exclusively to us. But for Pier Giorgio prayer was not a way of escaping reality. On the contrary, it enabled him to become ever more present to reality—a permanent incarnation within us and around us. In this way, Pier Giorgio wrote to two friends who had just lost a loved one: *"Our shared faith in Jesus Christ and our friendship allow me to participate in your great suffering. Instead of useless speeches, I offer my prayers"* (August 29, 1924).

His prayers of intercession always made him more sensitive and attentive to the interior suffering of those around him. To them, he was a luminous presence in their darkest moments. One day, as his friends were boisterously crossing the college doorstep, Pier Giorgio alone noticed the great sadness etched on the face of one of the school supervisors. *"What's the matter, Ernesto?"* he asked. Ernesto's only son, aged fourteen, had just passed away. Pier Giorgio stayed by his side in silence. Exactly one year later, he approached the supervisor again: *"Today is the anniversary of your son's death,"* he whispered; *"I will pray for him during Communion"* (LFJ 70). Such deep kindness stunned Ernesto.

Dear Pier Giorgio, you inclined your heart to charity, giving yourself completely to the poor and the sick. May the Lord give me strength to act effectively for the sake of the weakest. Despite criticism and mockery, you kept your appetite for true happiness; may it free me from the fear of failure. You sought the truth in the Lord; may he guide me along that demanding path and show me how to build beautiful and lasting friendships. As the lead climber, may you guide me to the heights, all the way to our Savior Jesus Christ. *Verso l'alto!*

Discussion Questions

Do I pray every day? What styles of prayer work well for me and which are more challenging? Why?

Who are my favorite saints and how do I cultivate my friendship with them?

If someone asks me how to pray, what would I advise them?

Have I had any prayers answered in surprising ways?

Also available in the
"15 Days of Prayer" series:

Blessed Chiara Badano, Florence Gillet
978-1-56548-554-9, paper

Brother Roger of Taize, Sabine Laplane
978-1-56548-349-1, paper
978-1-56548-375-0, ebook

Chiara Lubich, Florence Gillet
978-1-56548-513-6, Paper

Peter Joseph Triest, René Stockman
978-1-56548-700-0, paper

Saint Faustina Kowalska, John J. Cleary
978-1-56548-350-7, paper
978-1-56548-499-3, ebook

Saint Thérèse of Lisieux, Constant Tonnelier
978-1-56548-391-0, paper
978-1-56548-436-8, ebook

FOCOLARE MEDIA

Enkindling the Spirit of Unity

The New City Press book you are holding in your hands is one of the many resources produced by Focolare Media, which is a ministry of the Focolare Movement in North America. The Focolare is a worldwide community of people who feel called to bring about the realization of Jesus' prayer: "That all may be one" (see John 17:21).

Focolare Media wants to be your primary resource for connecting with people, ideas, and practices that build unity. Our mission is to provide content that empowers people to grow spiritually, improve relationships, engage in dialogue, and foster collaboration within the Church and throughout society.

Visit www.focolaremedia.com to learn more about all of New City Press's books, our award-winning magazine *Living City*, videos, podcasts, events, and free resources.

NCP
NEW CITY PRESS

www.ingramcontent.com/pod-product-compliance
Lightning Source LLC
LaVergne TN
LVHW021523080426
835509LV00018B/2623